Nido R. Qubein

Communicate Like a Pro

A SPECTRUM BOOK

Prentice-Hall, Inc., Englewood Cliffs, New Jersey 07632

Library of Congress Cataloging in Publication Data

Qubein, Nido R.
   Communicate like a pro.

   "A Spectrum Book."
   Includes index.
   1. Communication.   I. Title.
P90.Q39   1983   001.54   83–11135
ISBN 0–13–153734–2
ISBN 0–13–153726–1 (pbk.)

To my son, Ramsey, with love.

© 1983 by Nido R. Qubein

This book is available at a special discount when ordered
in bulk quantities. Contact Prentice-Hall, Inc., General
Publishing Division, Special Sales, Englewood Cliffs, N.J. 07632.

1 2 3 4 5 6 7 8 9 10

ISBN 0-13-153734-2

ISBN 0-13-153726-1 {PBK.}

Editorial production/supervision by Rita Young
Cover design © 1983 by Jeannette Jacobs
Manufacturing buyer: Pat Mahoney

Prentice-Hall International, Inc., *London*
Prentice-Hall of Australia Pty. Limited, *Sydney*
Prentice-Hall Canada Inc., *Toronto*
Prentice-Hall of India Private Limited, *New Delhi*
Prentice-Hall of Japan, Inc., *Tokyo*
Prentice-Hall of Southeast Asia Pte. Ltd., *Singapore*
Whitehall Books Limited, *Wellington, New Zealand*
Editora Prentice-Hall do Brasil Ltda., *Rio de Janeiro*

CONTENTS

PREFACE

Communicate Like a Pro starts with a glimpse into how professional communicators connect with their audiences. The principles for connecting with an audience are the same whether you are speaking to a loved one, addressing an audience of a thousand people, writing an article for publication, or negotiating an international arms reduction treaty.

Chapters 1 through 6 of the book offer suggestions and give techniques for establishing and maintaining contact with your audience. I show how involving my audiences has made me one of the most popular professional speakers in America, and how you can use the same principles and techniques to convey all kinds of messages through a wide variety of media.

Chapters 7 through 10 focus on the actual process of sending messages that produce desired responses. Separate chapters offer insights for each of the following questions: "Who do you wish to reach?" "What do you wish them to do?" "How will you get them to do it?" and "How will you know when they do it?"

Chapters 11 through 17 of the book give practical guidance on how to apply the principles of effective communication to the various "vehicles of communication." Such topics as using nonverbal signals, humor and visual aids, and developing your own style are discussed in simple, practical terms.

Tips are offered in such areas as: How to get the most out of personal contacts; how to use the telephone effectively; how to hold productive meetings; how to speak to a group like a pro; how to write effective letters, memos and notices; how to write for publication; and how to communicate through broadcast media.

Simple, easy-to-understand words, many verbal illustrations, and constant efforts to draw the reader into the subject, make this a very attractive book for individual readers and for use in groups. "Growth Exercises," at the end of each chapter, will help you to apply the ideas and techniques discussed to your own area of communication.

Communicate Like a Pro speaks to one of the most crucial aspects of human relationships—effective communication. Read, learn, and enjoy.

ACKNOWLEDGMENTS

My thanks to the hundreds of meeting planners who engaged me to motivate, educate, and inspire their audiences . . . and to the millions of individuals who have read my books, learned from my cassette programs, heard me on radio over the years, and attended my speeches and seminars. This book is a result of these experiences.

I am grateful to Robert I. Smith, who first suggested that I record and nationally syndicate a daily radio program—and then helped me to do it. I am also grateful to Margie and DuPree Jordan, who heard me when I was a novice speaker but believed in me nevertheless and proceeded to send scores of speaking engagements my way; to Ben B. Franklin who early on booked me to speak more than 100 times to Executive Club dinners from coast to coast; and to my associate Tom Watson, without whom the research for this book would have been impossible to complete.

Also, I am indebted to my family and my staff who have patiently endured my long trips and my exhausting work schedules— and throughout our time together have continued to give me unending support.

Finally, I'd like to communicate my appreciation to all my colleagues at the National Speakers Association who elected me as their president; to the business and professional leaders who helped me in establishing the Nido Qubein Associates Scholarship Fund to educate deserving young people; to my talented partners in the Professional Speakers Group; to my pals in the Furnitureland Rotary Club; and to my hometown folk in High Point, North Carolina, who have believed in me and supported me so enthusiastically during the past decade.

CHAPTER ONE

HOW YOU CAN BECOME A MORE EFFECTIVE COMMUNICATOR

This book is for you if:

- You feel your success and personal happiness depend on your effectiveness in communicating with audiences of 1 to 1,000.
- You ever say something you don't mean, or fail to say something you mean.
- Your signals are ever misunderstood, misinterpreted, or ignored.
- You ever have difficulty in gaining or holding attention from those with whom you want to communicate.
- You want to put power in your persuasion.
- You feel you waste a lot of time with unnecessary or unproductive communications attempts.

Communications take place between humans—you can't communicate with a computer. Communications have to do with meanings, with understandings, with feelings, with desires, with needs, with ideas—computers only store and process data. Only people have needs, desires, ideas, and feelings; and the capacity to understand, to think, to attach meanings to images and symbols.

Marshall McLuhan was dead right about many things: the world has become a global village connected by radio waves and television satellites; the media do influence everything we do and think; and they are playing a significant role in the unfolding of history. But the professor's claim that "the medium is the message"

1

is true only to the extent that communicators become lazy, un-skilled, and ineffective.

As a professional speaker, consultant to industry leaders, and a businessman, I have learned the power of effective communication to influence the actions and attitudes of individuals and audiences of thousands.

And as a human being, a husband, a father, and a friend, I have seen the tremendous impact of effectiveness in communicating on the relationships with significant persons who make my life worth living.

Effective communicators have said things to me that have:

- Encouraged me when I was near defeat.
- Inspired me to become more than I had been.
- Equipped me to become more successful, happier, and a better person.
- Corrected me when I was in error.
- Stimulated me to act on countless occasions.
- Given me ideas that I could build upon.
- Directed me when I was lost or confused.
- Amused me and brought joy to my life.
- Enriched my life.
- Helped me sort out problems and find solutions.

I'd bet you could say the same things about effective communicators who have touched your life. And I'd also bet you have discovered, as I have, that each of us can touch the lives of others in many ways through effective communication:

- We can get them to do things we want them to do.
- We can help them understand ideas and meanings that are important to us and them.
- We can change the course of their lives.
- We can get them to like us, and to respond favorably to us.
- We can lift their spirits, give them hope, and bring them comfort.
- We can sell them products or services.
- We can strengthen their self-images and boost their self-confidence.

Our powers to influence the lives of others and the world around us are great as are our abilities to communicate.

FIVE KEYS THAT CAN MAKE YOU
A MORE EFFECTIVE COMMUNICATOR

There's a common myth which holds that some people are born effective communicators, and others are not—that those who communicate well do so because they have that innate ability, and those who don't do it well lack those inborn traits and skills that enable them to touch the lives of others.

As you think about some of the great communicators of the last half century, it might be easy to conclude that people such as Franklin D. Roosevelt, Winston Churchill, John F. Kennedy, the Rev. Billy Graham, and others are natural-born communicators. Yet, each of them had to work hard at it; and many of the most skilled communicators had to overcome severe handicaps to even be able to convey the simplest messages. For example, did you know that Roosevelt inspired strength and courage in a whole nation from a wheelchair, or that Churchill had a severe speech impediment that made extensive speech therapy necessary during his childhood and early adulthood?

The fact is that you can become an effective communicator even if you are now very poor at it. And you can become more effective at communicating even if you are already considered an outstanding communicator.

Maybe your reasons for reading this book are simple: you're tired of having your letters ignored, or you want to be able to get what you order in a restaurant, or you want to be able to get a date. Or maybe your reasons are more ambitious: you want to become an effective public speaker, you want to boost your selling power and income, or perhaps you are a minister and you want to influence more effectively the lives in your congregation.

Whatever your reasons, there are five keys that can unlock your potential as an effective communicator.

KEY # 1: DESIRE

If you want to badly enough, you can become an effective communicator. The question is: how badly do you want to become really good at it?

"I'd give anything to be able to speak to an audience as effectively as you do!" people sometimes say to me after I have given a keynote speech or conducted a seminar. "You'd be ten times better than I if you'd invest one-tenth of what I have invested," I usually reply.

Sometimes I tell them the story of the Greek orator Demosthenes. Demosthenes lived in what is often called the "golden age of orators," in a land where all public disputes were settled by public oration. Once when he was a young man, he asked to speak to the assembly and was granted a hearing on a vital issue. His weak voice trembled as he began to speak, his thoughts were muddled, and he became more frightened as the speech progressed. Finally, his speech was disrupted with boos and hisses, and he was forced to step down. Humiliated, he withdrew from public life.

But Demosthenes was not so easily defeated. You see, he wanted more than anything to be a great orator. So to improve his diction, he practiced for hours at a time with stones in his mouth. To strengthen his weak voice, he shouted for hours at a time into the heavy winds coming off the Aegean Sea. To clarify his presentation, he studied the techniques of the masters. And to overcome his fears, he practiced with a sword hanging over his head.

When the next opportunity came along years later, he was ready. He stepped to the front of the assembly to warn the national leaders of the great threat posed by Philip II of Macedonia and to offer practical ideas as to how they should fight against this dangerous intruder. So powerful was his speech and so clear were his thoughts that, when he had finished, the entire audience rose as one person and began to shout, "Let us go and fight Philip!"

Even today, great speakers and historians study the speeches of Demosthenes—not because he was a born communicator, nor because he had great teachers—but because he had a burning desire to communicate effectively.

KEY #2: UNDERSTAND THE PROCESS OF COMMUNICATING

When I first came to America as a young man, I felt like an alien from a strange planet. I knew almost no English, nothing of the customs and traditions of the people in my new homeland, and virtually no one. That's quite a cultural shock for a person who had been a successful communicator and had been surrounded by friends and family. Adding to my challenge, my driving ambition was to become an effective communicator.

The only things going for me were the strong desire to communicate and the belief that the process of communicating was the same in every language, in every culture, and in every country on the face of the earth.

The process of communicating is basically *sending and receiving images.* We tend to think in images or pictures. To communicate those images to others we rely on vehicles such as words, pictures, sounds, and gestures. We use the same means whether we are trying to catch a waiter's attention to order another cup of coffee or trying to explain Einstein's theory of relativity to a group of college students.

Of course, the real challenge is to send accurate images to others, as well as receive accurate images from them: to convey things exactly as you see them, and to receive them exactly as others see them. Those tasks are complicated by our God-given abilities, as individuals, to send and receive very complex images, to relate them to other images we have captured in our memories, and to attach meanings to the images we receive and retain—but more about that in a later chapter.

I like to think of communicating as *mind-to-mind reorientation.* In other words, when you communicate effectively you can change the way people think, feel, and act by enabling them to understand the way you think, feel and act. And if you are a good listener, you can reverse that process.

Now, believing that that process is the same in any country, or culture, or language, I set about to communicate as best I could with the people in my strange new land. It worked well—though it was difficult—and it led me to the next key to unlocking my potential as an effective communicator.

KEY #3: MASTER
CERTAIN BASIC SKILLS

Almost every book I've ever read on various aspects of communication has focused on the mechanics of communicating, like building a large vocabulary, learning how to structure coherent sentences, and voice modulation. If I had relied upon them, it would have been years before I could have gotten started—and I couldn't wait. I was broke, I was lonely, and I was challenged by the new people I was meeting.

The basic skills that launched me on what has proved to be a very successful professional speaking career were these: connecting with an audience, conveying messages they could understand, and checking their responses.

How did I do that? I pulled out some slides I brought from my native country and put together a slide show on "Easter in the Holy Land," borrowed a projector, and started doing my little program for every church and civic group that would grant me an audience. Since Easter was coming up soon, many groups invited me.

To connect with those audiences, I would tell stories—in my broken English—about what it was like to learn their strange customs. I talked about learning how to drive, getting accustomed to "strange foods" like hamburgers, giving someone a complete rundown on my physical condition when they asked, "How are you?" and going back and saying, "What do you want?" after the clerk in a store as a sign of courtesy said, "Come back!" as I started out the door. Those people would nearly roll in the floor with laughter as I stumbled through such stories.

Not only were they amused, they got very involved with what I was saying. I would have to stop periodically and ask, "How do you say it . . . ?" They would work hard at trying to put words into my mouth, and they hung onto every word I said or sought.

To convey messages in an unfamiliar language, I relied on pictures and simple descriptions of scenes as familiar to me as the back of my hand. A picture of a small ass standing beside a magnificent horse conveyed more adequately the humility of Jesus' triumphal entry into Jerusalem much better than I could have depicted it by means of my broken English.

Checking audience response was a matter of asking for questions as I went along. This not only helped me stretch out my short presentation, it helped me to monitor their interest level and to key my comments to their areas of greatest interest.

After many years of speaking to audiences, I don't use slides anymore, but I still rely very heavily upon those skills of connecting with my audience, conveying messages they understand, and constantly checking their responses. My topics now cover a broad range of subjects that touch the most vital issues of human endeavor, my presentations are now highly polished, and I use very sophisticated techniques to accomplish my goals. All that has been possible because I have never forgotten the basic skills I've outlined here, and because I have used the next master key to effective communication.

KEY #4: PRACTICE

Those early "shows" would stimulate my audiences to take up small offerings for me, which enabled me to work my way through college, but they certainly could not have satisfied my needs as a human being, nor could they have offered me a very lucrative career. Given my driving personality, and the economic realities of life, I had to move on to bigger and better things—I had to become an effective communicator.

To accomplish that, I made practicing a way of life. Part of the inspiration for that came from a story I heard about a young musician who approached an old master who had just completed the most beautiful rendition of a complex collection of great compositions he'd ever heard.

"Sir," the young man said admiringly, "It must be great to have all the practicing behind you and be able to simply sit down and play like that."

"Oh!" the old master replied, "I still practice eight hours every day."

"But, why? I mean . . . you are so good!" exclaimed the young musician.

"I wish to become superb!" answered the old master.

Now, as I train thousands of people each year in various forms of communication, I find that most of them are quite satisfied to become "good." Few, very few, are willing to invest the countless hours of practicing that are required to become "superb."

Mastery of the basic skills of connecting, conveying, and checking response comes only with practice; and the skillful use of the techniques for doing that—which I shall present in the remainder of this book—comes only after hours of refinement through drilling, drilling, and more drilling.

And, that brings me to the final key I've discovered from a lifetime of studying the great masters at effective communication.

Very early, I realized that people found my mumbling, stumbling presentations amusing because I was a young college student, making the best of my strange new environment. Had I continued in my ineptness as a speaker, they would have soon felt sorry for me; those who gave me a chance because they saw me trying so hard would have tuned me out because I wasn't making progress.

You see, children are attractive to us precisely because they are growing. When a two-year-old mispronounces words, uses the wrong words, and gets frustrated because he or she can't find the right words, we find it amusing. But, if that same person is still doing those things at the age of thirty, we think of them as being "retarded," or "mentally disturbed." It is a fact of life that we must grow, or we begin to wither up and die.

But there is another very real fact of life—growth takes time! At least it does for humans. A horse can become independent from its mother within a year, and be put to work as a full-grown draft horse within three years. Likewise, a dog can begin "house training" within a month or two after birth. But it is not so for human beings; they develop much more slowly.

That growing process is often painfully slow. It's like the fifteen-year-old boy who almost hates his parents because they won't let him have the car until he's licensed—and that can only happen when he's sixteen. Or, like the twelve-year-old girl in a seminar for youth who, feeling the loneliness of being suspended between childhood and the teen years, shouted, "I feel like I'm nothing but a frog!"

Go as hard as you can go, learn as many techniques of communicating as you can, and practice all you will; it still takes time to become an effective communicator. The older I get, the more I admire the Norman Vincent Peales, the Earl Nightengales, and the Paul Harveys who have blazed the trail before me in the professional speaking field. If I can learn half of what they know, I can raise my effectiveness as a communicator to a level beyond my wildest dreams of a few years ago.

But they didn't become mature, effective communicators overnight. Nor will I; nor will you. It takes patience—the patience of giving it all you've got while waiting for what you acquire to mature.

There's more to this process of maturing as an effective communicator than patience: you must be willing to subject yourself to ruthless self-evaluation. When your communication attempts fail, you must not only be willing to admit that they have failed; you must be willing to search out why they failed.

Many years ago, I visited St. Peter's Cathedral, in Rome and was overwhelmed by the huge, life-like statues which showed the masterful skill of Michelangelo. I was particularly awed by the realism conveyed by the gigantic image of Moses. Now, I thought to myself, that sculptor was a master at communicating.

Then I noticed a chipped place on one of the knees of the statue. Disturbed that anyone could have been so careless as to damage such a life-like image, I asked the guide how it had happened.

"The scar was put there by the artist himself," she replied. "When he finished the statue, it is said that he backed away from it, looked at it for a long time, then threw a hammer at it screaming, 'Why dost thou not speak?'," she explained.

It occurred to me later that there is a little of that in all of the great communicators I have known and studied. They are not so overwhelmed by their feelings of inferiority that they cannot question their best efforts; nor are they so smug in the compliments of others that they cannot call failure what others have called success. No matter what they do, or how well they do it, they always search for a better way of doing it in the future.

There is a thin line between destructive self-criticism which destroys self-confidence and constructive self-criticism which spurs you on to try harder. No one can define that line for you; it's something you must find for yourself. But those who find it can become increasingly effective communicators.

TYING IT ALL TOGETHER

We have seen that effective communication can increase your productivity, enrich your relationships, and enable you to have an impact on the lives of others and on the world around you.

And we have seen that the process of communicating is basically simple: it is a matter of connecting with an audience (whether it's an audience of 1 or 1,000), conveying images that audience can understand, and checking constantly the responses of that audience. In other words, communicating is a matter of sending and receiving images.

But we have also seen that becoming an effective communicator requires: desire, understanding of the basic process, mastery of certain basic skills, practice, and patience.

You have a strong desire to become an effective, or more effective, communicator, or you would not have read this entire first chapter. If you will stay with me for the remainder of this book, you will be able to raise the level of your effectiveness more than enough to justify the time it requires.

Before we move on to examine together the basic skills, techniques, and tools of communicating, pause a moment and do the "Growth Exercise" below. (You'll find one of these exercises at the end of each chapter; it will help you think about what we have discussed in that chapter.)

GROWTH EXERCISE

Think, for a moment, about the most recent occasion when a writer or speaker deeply moved you—moved you to act or change your feelings about an issue.

Now, answer each of the following questions:

1. How did the communicator connect with me? By what means did that person get and hold my attention?
2. How did the communicator convey images that I came to understand—perhaps for the first time?
3. Was I aware of attempts by the communicator to check my responses? If so, how?

CHAPTER TWO

THE HIGH ART
OF CONNECTING
WITH YOUR AUDIENCE

Do you know who Edward Everett was?

If you don't readily recall the name, I'm sure you'll recall the occasion of his most famous speech. He spoke in Gettysburg, PA, on November 19, 1863, at the dedication of a national cemetery.

Everett was considered a genius. He graduated from Harvard at seventeen, studied abroad, and had an extraordinary memory. And, he is listed in encyclopedias as one of the greatest orators of the nineteenth century. He had arrived in Gettysburg days before he was to give the speech, just to study the people and prepare his speech. When he stepped to the speaker's platform on the day for the dedication, a hush fell across the audience. His dignified manner, his carefully organized remarks, and his brilliant style and delivery held the attention of his audience for more than an hour.

But there was another speaker in the little Pennsylvania town that day, a man so awkward in appearance that he was often characterized as baboon-like, and was considered by some to be an embarrassment to his country. Because of the press of his duties, he had had little time to prepare—he'd only jotted down a few notes (some historians say on a napkin) on the brief train ride from Washington that day.

As that second speaker strolled to the podium, there was no smile for the audience, no humorous stories, no heart-warming illustrations. His speech contained only 266 words and lasted less than five minutes.

"Fourscore and seven years ago . . ." the speaker started; and the rest is so familiar that almost every fifth-grade student in America can recite it for you. The second speaker was Abraham Lincoln, and his message was the famous "Gettysburg Address."

Lincoln's remarks touched the hearts of the people; it spoke to their needs, their dreams, their fears, their hurts. When he had finished, there wasn't a dry eye in the audience—including the eyes of the first speaker.

What made the difference? Why do we remember that second speech more than a century later, while only historians can tell us what Edward Everett said that day?

AN ANATOMY OF A CLASSIC

Abraham Lincoln's "Gettysburg Address" was a classic because:

It was the right person,
Saying the right thing,
To the right people,
At the right place,
At the right time,
In the right way.
It was heard and understood,
And it produced the desired effect.
That, essentially, is *effective communication.*

There is a common mark by which you can identify all classic examples of effective communication: the communicators all connected with their audiences.

Think for a moment about your own successful attempts to communicate with other people. Maybe what comes first to mind is the time you first said "I love you" to a person who now occupies a significant place in your life. Maybe it was a job interview that opened the door to a great opportunity for you. Or, perhaps, you spoke to a large audience and felt them breathing with you.

Whatever comes to mind as a high moment in your communication experience, one thing is certain: it was a moment when you connected with your audience.

Do you feel you could be more successful in your career and

enrich your personal relationships if you could increase the frequency with which you really connect with your audiences? If so, you are absolutely right.

But how do you do that? How do you become the right person, saying the right thing, to the right people, at the right place, at the right time, in the right way to be heard, and understood? How do you increase the frequency with which you really connect with your audiences? You must keep in mind that one thing must precede any effort to understand the techniques and tools of effective communication: nothing matters more than the speaker's attitude!

ALL EFFECTIVE COMMUNICATION IS DIALOG

There's a new word in our thinking together about communication: dialog. What does it mean? Let me give you the definition that has worked best for me: Dialog is what happens when the reality within you, contacts the reality within your audience, and, together, you move toward a common new reality.

Dialog is not only essential to effective communication, it is essential to life. The human race has become so interdependent that our survival depends on our ability to relate to each other.

This drama of survival through dialog is played out thousands of times every moment around the world. Let me illustrate.

"Scalpel!" says the doctor in the operating room.

"Scalpel!" replies the nurse.

The success of the operation, as well as the survival of the patient, rest squarely on the accurate sending and receiving of messages between that doctor and nurse.

Of course, not all dialog is that dramatic, but it is nonetheless essential to the people involved. The "goodbye kiss" which holds out the hope of a return, the signed labor agreement that keeps people working, the international treaty that moves nations from the brink of nuclear disaster—all represent dialog. Our personal happiness, our earning a living, even our existence as a race depend on our abilities to communicate effectively—to engage others in dialog.

Every person (or group of persons) we meet is potentially our friend, and potentially our enemy. What determines the differ-

13

ence is our willingness and ability to engage the people who touch our lives in dialog.

Peter Sellers dramatized the results of a failure in dialog in his famous movie, "Doctor Strangelove." This powerful satire on the nuclear madness focused for millions of people how the world could be literally blown apart when the process of dialog breaks down.

In everyday life, failure to communicate effectively is played out in broken hearts, muggings, and lost jobs. Again, let me illustrate.

Star Daily became the most notorious criminal in England early in this century. He wasn't always a vicious killer, ruthless armed robber, and hardened person. The four decades of terror he poured out on every community he visited began when he was a small boy in a classroom. The teacher routinely called upon him to stand in front of the class and read a simple passage.

Timidly, the little boy stepped to the front of the room, took the book from the teacher, and began to stumble through the passage. The harder he tried, the more the words ran together; and the more frightened he became, and the more he stumbled. Snickers from the other students began to bounce through the room. Gradually they turned to giggles, then open laughter.

Hurt and afraid, young Star looked to his older sister who was also in the class. Surely, since she was his only living relative after his parents died a few years earlier, she would understand, he hoped. But her head was buried in her arms on her desk, and she too was laughing.

In desperation, he turned to the only potential source of comfort left in the classroom: his teacher. Just as his eyes met hers, she put her handkerchief to her mouth to stifle the laugh she had been holding in. He was crushed.

Suddenly, the timid little boy exploded with rage! He slammed the book shut, threw it with all his strength against the opposite wall, and ran toward the door.

"You will fear me! You will hate me! But, never again will you laugh at me!" he shouted as he paused at the door. He ran from that class, from that school, from that town. And as he ran, he pillaged and killed everywhere he went until the end of his life.

Juvenile delinquents and criminals don't become losers the

first time they are caught. They've been losers all their lives. Somehow, they have not been able to engage in the dialog that enables them to see themselves as lovable and capable members of our society. They have not been able to make significant contact with persons who could affirm their worth as human beings. In addition, those around them have failed in their efforts at reaching out to touch them through the dialog of love.

DIALOG TOUCHES
EVERY AREA OF OUR LIVES

Look at the geniuses of recent history, and ask yourself what it was that separated them from other people who were born "brilliant," but whose names we have never heard. More often than not, their greatness—and certainly the value of their contributions—lay in their abilities to translate what they saw to other people.

- Thomas A. Edison was noted for his ability to use assistants in his laboratories to help him sort through the endless experiments needed to lead to his great discoveries. He was able to communicate to them what he was hoping to find and to inspire them to search with him.
- Albert Einstein once said, "The whole of science is nothing more than a refinement of everyday thinking." He frequently engaged in dialog to keep in touch with that "everyday thinking."
- Henry Ford's genius lay, not so much in his concept of an automobile (countless others "invented" fine automobiles), nor even in his ingenious plan for the assembly line. His true contribution came from his unique ability to get other people to do things.

Perhaps the most notable communicator of our present age is Dr. Martin Luther King, who touched the conscience of the nation by means of the new medium of television. His reasoning was simple: if he could make people "see" the dogs tearing the flesh from black people in Montgomery, let them "feel" the hatred on the road to Selma, and "touch" the deep longings of people for freedom, the collective conscience of this nation would be stirred to action. History has proved that he was right.

Dialog can be as non-verbal as a hand on the shoulder of a

grieving friend when words seem inadequate, or as verbal as a lawyer's plea to a jury. It can be as spontaneous as a cry for help from a victim trapped in a fire, or as rehearsed as an inaugural address by a president. And it can be as simple as a smile, or as complex as a lecture on nuclear physics. Whatever its form, it becomes dialog only when it connects with its intended audience.

THE CRISIS IN DIALOG

Ours is the most connected world in history. Each night, we are connected with people who are survivors of a flood in Ohio, or a war in the Middle East, or a dictatorship in South America, or starvation in Africa. We are bombarded by reports on radio, in newspapers and magazines, and on the ever-present television screen.

Yet, with all this connection, sociologists are calling this the most disconnected generation of history. They speak of a loss of intimacy between persons, and general feelings of alienation.

Psychologists are talking increasingly about "skin-touch anemia," and medical doctors are now claiming that more than half of all physical problems have their origin in deep-seated personal unhappiness, stress, and anxiety.

People are having more and more trouble getting into significant contact with each other. You sense it when you walk into a convenience store, and the clerk looks right through you as he or she rings up your purchase. You feel it when you watch the empty stares of the young people who dance alone—in a crowd—on "American Bandstand." You notice it in the blank stares of people in airports, on busy avenues, and in large stadiums.

It's as if we have become a nation of spectators. There's so much input coming at us, from so many sources and directions, that we have to filter out what we don't want to see and hear just to survive emotionally and intellectually. We develop those filters to protect us from sensory and intellectual overload.

Just as we learn to flip the selector on our television set to tune out programming that doesn't interest us, we learn to "tune out" people whom we don't wish to engage us in dialog. It's a matter of survival.

So we become masters at "monolog in duet," where I think

up what I'm going to say while you're saying what you thought up while I was talking. We are fighting the habit of "monologue in duet" every time we try to sell a prospect who is preoccupied with personal concerns, or attempt to speak to a large audience which has been sitting too long, or try to get a letter to jump out from the mammoth stack of "junk mail" on a busy executive's desk.

As a result, if you want to become an effective communicator, you must learn how to break through that highly-refined mental "tune-out" device that most people have developed to protect themselves from people like you.

THE LAW OF EFFECTIVE COMMUNICATION

There is only one way to avoid that "tune-out" device. Keep in mind my first law of effective communication: No worthwhile communication can take place until you gain the complete attention of your audience, and, at the moment you lose that attention, effective communication stops.

In other words, talking when nobody is listening is as futile as trying to cut paper with half a pair of scissors. Response is the only thing that can transform words or images into dialog.

It is important to realize that if your intent is to "make a good speech," or "write a good letter," or "give instructions no one could misunderstand," you have missed the most important element of effective communication: gaining and holding the attention of the audience. Good speeches, good letters, and clear instructions are important—as we shall see later—but it is more important to connect with the person with whom you wish to communicate.

Shortly after I was elected president of the National Speakers Association, a reporter asked me my secret formula for professional success.

I replied that I managed to stay busy because so many organizations and people invite me back for return engagements.

"But why do they invite you back?" he asked, adding, "Once was enough for most of the speakers I've heard."

"Probably it's because to me the audience is top priority," I said.

"What do you mean?" he persisted.

"The very first thing I do when I'm introduced is get the audience into the act. I get them to do something with me," I explained. "I only proceed with my talk when I'm sure I've got their undivided attention and, if at any moment I feel I have lost their attention, I do something to re-establish that contact."

GET PERSONAL, GAIN ATTENTION

Messages become interesting to us—and thereby gain our attention—only when they become very personal to us. For example, if I asked you to read through an airline schedule you'd probably shrug it off as too boring to even consider. On the other hand, if you were planning to take a whirlwind tour of the world, and you only had a limited time to travel, an airline schedule would probably become very interesting to you.

Another instance is the way you read a newspaper. Perhaps you skim through the headlines to see what affects you, or coincides with your own experiences. You might throw away whole sections which don't in any way touch your personal life. You are drawn to particular columns, particular features. If you own stocks, you probably check out how those stocks did in the most recent trading; and if you're a farmer, you might check out wholesale crop prices. ("You know you're getting old," said an aging friend to me, "when the first thing you read is the obituary columns.")

The real professionals in this business of communicating are very sensitive to this principle of finding out what interests people. Politicians spend a fortune before every election trying to determine through polls exactly what the people in their constituency are thinking about the major issues they confront. The television networks are no longer satisfied in knowing how many people watch a particular show: they want to know who is watching (the rating services give them a complete demographic breakdown of the audience by age, sex, locality, and income bracket) and why they are watching.

To one who wants to become a more effective communicator, nothing should matter more than raising your audience-response potential—which is the subject of our next chapter.

TYING IT ALL TOGETHER

Communication occurs when the right person, says the right thing, to the right people, at the right place, at the right time, and in the right way to be heard and understood, and to produce the desired response.

All effective communication is dialog which happens when the reality within one person touches the reality within another person or persons, and together they move toward a new, shared reality.

Dialog is essential, not only to effective communication, but to every area of our lives. If we are to become effective at dialog, we must find ways to break through the "tune-out" devices which people in our audiences have developed to protect themselves from sensory and intellectual overloads.

We can only communicate effectively when we have the attention of our audience, and that can best be gained through becoming personal with those with whom we would communicate.

GROWTH EXERCISE

Listen carefully to a radio commercial and analyze it carefully to determine each of the following things:

1. How did the commercial's producers attempt to gain your attention?
2. Did their strategy work on you? If so, why? If not, why not?
3. What appeal was made to get you personally involved?
4. Did you think the commercial gained the attention of the audience for which it was intended? Why? Why not?
5. Based on the ideas we have presented in this chapter how could the commercial been done more effectively?

CHAPTER THREE

HOW TO BOOST YOUR AUDIENCE-RESPONSE RATING

Effective communicators are good company; they're interesting to be around. They make you feel special, like you're really somebody. They're interested in you, in what you do, in what you think, and how you feel.

It's not so much that they make you like them—although they often do that—but it's more that they make you like yourself or, at least, make you feel like you're worth something.

Or they might make you want to be more than you are. It might even make you feel ashamed to be the way you are when you sense that the reality in them is greater than the reality in you. But they get away with it because they accept you for what you are and invite you to go on with them to become more of what you can be.

Nobody likes to be around a bore. Listening to a bore reminds me of what someone said about Edward Everett (the orator mentioned in the last chapter) and how it felt to be in an audience where he was speaking. "When you hear him," said a critic, "you button your coat to keep from taking a cold."

I'm sure you know people like that. They're always talking about themselves and what they've done; they're always talking about "great ideas" while you're thinking about great problems— or maybe they're always talking about their problems while you're trying to think about great ideas. The big problem is that they don't seem to care what you are thinking about, or feeling, or interested in.

What's the difference? Why is it that you can't wait until some speakers finish while you wish others would keep going for hours?

WHAT IS AUDIENCE-RESPONSE POTENTIAL?

Those who communicate like pros have *audience-response potential.* They have the ability to connect with an audience, and get that audience to connect with them. In the entertainment business they call it "stage presence," that intangible charisma that causes an audience to sit up and take notice when the performer comes on stage; that subtle difference that causes an audience to pick out a particular performer to watch when the stage is full of people.

Look, for example, at Diana Ross, the singer. It's not just that she feels the music so deeply. The "cat" who "grooves" down the street with his "box" (translated radio) feels the music perhaps just as deeply. No, it's more than that. Diana Ross has the ability to make the audience feel the music with her.

Rev. Robert Schuller does the same thing with his sermons and speeches, though they are in a different vein. He has the ability to get groups of people to join with him in "possibility thinking." Evangelist Oral Roberts has inspired millions of people to practice "seed faith." And Rev. Billy Graham has used his audience-response potential to get millions of people around the world to "make decisions for Christ." They all have that ability to make each person in an audience feel as though he is being addressed individually.

Writers do it, too. Erma Bombeck has made a fortune by getting into the minds of people and reflecting back to them, in a humorous way, what they are thinking. Jack Anderson draws readers into his columns by asking the kinds of questions they'd like to ask of the people they'd like to interview. And *Jonathan Livingston Seagull* was a runaway best seller a few years ago because Richard Bach connected with the hopes and longings of millions of people.

Maybe you can't relate to any of the people I've named above, but I suspect you can connect with the fact that each of them has been highly successful as a communicator because of his ability to make and keep contact with a particular audience. They all communicate with millions of people—one person at a time.

HOW YOU CAN BOOST
YOUR AUDIENCE-RESPONSE RATING

Right now you might be thinking, "But those are all giants in their fields. . . . What about people like me who just want to be able to speak effectively to small groups or write letters that get answered?"

But what has made those people giants in their fields is that they have mastered the art of getting people to pay attention to them, which is exactly what any of us will have to do if we want to communicate effectively.

Some of the best advice I ever received was: "If you would be successful, study successful people. Learn what they do, and how they do it. Then, develop your own approach based on what has worked for others." Maybe you don't plan to become a syndicated columnist, or a television personality, or a motivational speaker. But, by studying the success strategies of the pros in those fields, you can become better at what you choose to do.

So, let's look carefully at some of the strategies the pros use to get people to pay attention to them.

STRATEGY #1: CULTIVATE
AUDIENCE SENSITIVITY

Poor communicators say what they think, and don't concern themselves with how their audience responds to it. For them, it's enough that "It's the truth!"

Average communicators say what they think, and watch the way people respond to it. They want what they say to be warmly received and acted upon.

But the *real pros* in communication check to see what their audiences think and feel, then appeal to those thoughts and feelings.

It's more than simply saying what you think people "want

to hear." Some of the real pros actually say things their audiences would rather not hear; but they never run roughshod over the feelings of the people that are listening to them.

All of us have "comfort zones" which we tend to protect from invaders who threaten us by the speed with which they approach, their manner of approach, and our perception of their intentions toward us. But we tend to readily receive those communicators who seem to care about us, and come to us with good will.

Someone once observed that there are two kinds of people in the world: guests and hosts. The guests tend to walk in, plop themselves down, and say, "Here I am . . . take care of me!" They are primarily concerned about their interests, their needs, their desires. And they make lousy communicators. But the hosts are sensitive to the feelings and needs of others. They concentrate on others, rather than always think about themselves. Their actions are designed to make others feel at home. And they have the potential for being great communicators.

Some of the real pros are natural hosts because of their temperament and personality, but others of them have worked hard to cultivate audience sensitivity. It's usually hard to tell, though, whether it comes naturally or is cultivated, because the people who are good at it do it with such finesse that you'd never know it takes effort.

Whether it's natural or cultivated, audience sensitivity has its impact—usually in subtle ways. For example, you won't find the pros talking down to an audience, or ignoring the physical needs of those who come to hear them, or cracking ethnic jokes that could offend people in the audience. They don't put people down, or criticize them in the presence of others, or try to make them look silly. Perhaps the best way to say it is that they have a sense of humanity, a feeling for the human touch. They seek to know their audiences as persons.

Try it sometime; you'll be amazed how well it works. The next time you visit a home where there's a four-year-old, sit right down on the floor and look the miniature human straight in the eyes. Speak as one person addressing another person—not as an adult addressing a child. Ask questions and listen—really listen—to responses. Make a big deal of everything the person shows you, or tells you. Pretty soon you'll be carrying on an interesting conversation. As it begins to develop, watch how the youngster opens up to you and becomes your friend. It really works!

You can try it on other people, on groups of people, even through correspondence. In fact, if you want to boost your audience-response rating, you must practice becoming sensitive to people until it becomes a habit with you. Stay with it until you can close your eyes and "feel" the presence of your audience.

Once you have become sensitive to your audience, you are ready for the next strategy for improving your audience-response rating.

STRATEGY #2: CULTIVATE AUDIENCE AWARENESS

Sensitivity and awareness are closely related, but they are not the same thing. Sensitivity has more to do with being responsive, being willing to observe and listen, being open to the needs and aspirations of your audience. But awareness is more assertive. The communicator with audience awareness stays active and alert in his or her involvement with that audience. It enables the communicator to set the pace for the dialog they wish to occur.

The real pros are so aware of their audiences that they can sense the slightest mood change, they can predict when interest will be at its peak, and they know when it's time to quit. This awareness gives them a feeling for timing, for pacing, for moving in for the close.

For example, when I write an important letter to a client, I try to determine when that letter will arrive at the person's office and what the client will most likely be doing when my letter comes to his or her attention. I've found that Monday morning is seldom a good time to try to communicate with a busy executive whose desk is full of other correspondence. Postal service makes it difficult to predict exactly when a letter will arrive, but I always try to make my proposals and requests arrive at the most convenient time for those to whom they are addressed.

The greater your awareness of what is going on with the person, or persons, with whom you want to communicate, the better are your chances for timing the messages you send for maximum effect. For instance, it does little good to give detailed instructions to an employee when that person is worried sick about a child facing a big operation. If you can wait until the crisis has passed or help the person deal with his or her feelings about the crisis before you give your instructions, your chances of being heard and getting the results you desire will be much greater.

I'm not suggesting that to be an effective communicator you have to rearrange your whole life for the convenience of all the people you seek to communicate with. What I am suggesting is that it always helps you to know how to send your messages in a way they are most likely to be received when you know what's going on with the people who will be receiving them. Let me illustrate. Many professional speakers have turned down attractive invitations to speak because they could only be scheduled in a time slot immediately following a huge cocktail party. No motivational speaker can be good enough to challenge an audience when most of its members are "soused."

With a little common sense and a cultivated sense of audience awareness, you can often predict quite accurately what impact your messages will produce. Thus, you can adjust your strategies to communicate more effectively.

To get a feeling for how this works, look at some non-fiction articles by writers in popular magazines. They anticipate which questions a statement or bit of information will raise in the minds of their readers. Notice how they use statements like: "Right now you're probably wondering . . ." or "Which raises the question . . ." or "As strange as it may seem . . ." It is obvious that they have a great awareness of what thoughts they are triggering in the minds of their readers.

My suggestion is, then, that if you want to boost your audience response rating you should cultivate an awareness of what is going on with the people you would address.

STRATEGY #3: SEEK TO UNDERSTAND YOUR AUDIENCE

Frank Bettger was one of the most successful salespeople and professional speakers who ever lived. His formula for success was simple: "Show people what they want and how to get it, and they will move Heaven and earth to get it."

One of the stories he told most often on his trips with Dale Carnegie was how he had sold two large insurance policies to a businessman who had met him at the door and told him "I quit buying insurance ten years ago."

According to Mr. Bettger, the man was nearing retirement and had seemingly covered every base with insurance: his family, his business, his personal property—everything.

"It is widely known in this community that you have been a very benevolent man," the old pro told his potential client. "I'd be curious to know which one of the charities you've been involved with over the years has meant the most to you."

A long conversation followed in which the man told him about his son and daughter-in-law who were missionaries in South America. Soon he was going to visit them in their field of labor. Also, he talked about a daughter and son-in-law doing the same work in another undeveloped country. Those missions, he mused, meant most to him because of his personal involvement with them.

"Wouldn't you like to be able to tell your son when you visit him that you have provided for his mission to receive a check each month so the work can go on, and he can continue to care for his little family, even after you have died?" asked Frank Bettger. "And, wouldn't you like to write a letter to your daughter and tell her the same thing?" he continued. "That's a great idea!" the man responded, pulling out his checkbook.

That old veteran made a sale—and made some people happy—by *understanding* his audience. He was able to show the man what he wanted, even though the man had not been aware that he wanted it, and the man was willing to do whatever was necessary to get it.

When you are sensitive to your audience and aware of your audience, it opens the door for you to understand your audience—and that opens the door to a greater audience-response rating.

You're simply wasting your time when you try to answer questions people are not asking. Even worse, you are wasting opportunities to communicate with others, and some of those opportunities will never come again.

To help them understand their audiences, the pros keep certain questions in their minds during all their attempts to communicate.

1. *What do they want out of life?* It's not just a matter of what they need, but a matter of how they perceive their needs and what they think it would take to satisfy their needs that helps you to understand. What motivates them, and what motivates them to do the opposite of what you want them to do?

I am often billed as a motivational speaker, but I'll let you in on a little secret. I can't motivate anybody! People do things for their own reasons—not for mine, nor for yours, nor for anyone else's. Furthermore, there are no "unmotivated" people. My audience might not be motivated to do what I want them to do or what you want them to do; but they are motivated to do what they want to do.

What I can do, and what I frequently do as a professional speaker, is to get in touch with what motivates them and channel their motivations along lines that are compatible with the goals of the organizations who invited me to speak. Also, I can—and do—help my audiences mobilize their resources to achieve the goals that matter to them. Perhaps that's why so many of my audiences respond favorably and so many of my sponsors invite me to return.

2. *What do they fear?* Effective communication often involves helping people overcome their fears, or steering clear of the things they fear. But there are times when effective communication requires the use of fears to get your point across.

Let's look at a couple of examples to see how this use of fear works. If someone is drowning, before you can pull the person from the water, you must first overcome his or her terror at the prospect of dying. When you have adequately communicated confidence that you can rescue the person, he or she will relax and let you pull them to shore. On the other hand, if you are trying to discourage someone from driving after they have been drinking, appealing to that fear of death might be a very effective technique.

The important point to remember is before you know how to deal with a person's fear, or the fears of an audience, you must understand what those fears are. The more you understand about what they fear, the more you can boost your audience-response rating.

3. *What do they know; what do they understand?* In some settings, jargon can be a great help in establishing contact with an audience, and it can help you cut through a lot of words to get right to the point. But if your audience doesn't understand your jargon, you will only confuse them and close the door to all communication. "All you need to know to teach a dog how to do tricks," the old saying goes, "is more than the dog knows." I would suggest to you that it is even more important to *know what the dog knows.*

"Proceed from the known, to the unknown" is an old axiom of educators. It is still good advice for people who want to be effective communicators. Getting in touch with what people know and understand can help you acquaint them with what they don't know.

One of the most helpful concepts for boosting your audience response rating is to do away with the old "caste system" which speaks of levels of understanding. Usually, the greater your expertise in a particular field, the more difficult it is for you to communicate effectively with anyone about that field—except for other experts. If you rate yourself *above* your audience, you will usually come across as condescending to them. Your goal in communicating is not to impress people with what you know, but to help them understand what you know to a point that they can act in the ways you want them to act. If you rate yourself as *below* them, on the other hand, you are likely to be intimidated by them. I have found that it is always more helpful to relate to myself as being *different* from my audiences, and to simply seek to understand what they know and don't know.

4. *What do they misunderstand?* This is the other side of the question we have just discussed, and it can pose some real obstacles to boosting your audience-response rating.

A friend of mine was once shopping for a bracelet as a gift in one of those stores that doesn't display the prices.

"That one looks real good," he said to the salesperson, "How much is it?"

"Four-fifty," came the casual reply as the customer was handed the bracelet for closer inspection.

"That's great!" replied my friend, "You don't think it will turn green on his arm, do you?"

"Well!" said the indignant clerk, "I should hope not!"

Both of them were very embarassed when he pulled out a five dollar bill to pay for a bracelet that cost four-hundred-fifty dollars. Needless to say, neither of them had picked up on what the other had misunderstood.

The real pros know that when people misunderstand the information they are being given or the communicator's motivation for giving it, they will throw up an impenetrable wall of resistance. If you want to boost your audience response rating, always stay alert for any misunderstanding, and deal with it properly.

STRATEGY #4: IDENTIFY WITH YOUR AUDIENCE

"Method" actors prepare for their roles by striving to "become" the persons they are trying to portray. Their goal is to be able to see the events they are trying to depict as if through the eyes of the characters they play.

Seeing the world through the eyes of other people is an excellent way to boost your audience-response rating. It's a simple ploy: the more you identify with the circumstances, needs, and feelings of your audience, the easier it is for your audience to identify with you.

When an audience is thinking "We think this, but you say that . . ." it is very hard to break through the walls of resistance and communicate very effectively. But when you become a part of their "we," and they sense you can identify with them, those walls come down.

Notice how many times Abraham Lincoln used the pronoun "we" in the Gettysburg Address, to which we referred earlier. No one in his audience would label the conflict which raged as "Abe's war" after he said, "*We* are engaged in this great civil war. . . ." And when Lincoln spoke of the soldiers whose bodies were in the cemetery he had come to dedicate in the presence of their loved ones, he said, "*We* have come to dedicate. . . ." As you read that speech, you could almost believe that the dead men were his brothers, or his sons, or his father. Contrast that with much of the "political rhetoric" that comes from government leaders today, and it's easy to see why so many people are becoming alienated from our nation's leaders. Many of them use terms like, "The American people are tired of . . ." or "Our polls indicate people want . . ." or "Those people who are on welfare. . . ." It is as if many would-be communicators are afraid they will lose their own identity if they identify with the feelings and needs of their audiences. "But our goals are not the same as those of our audiences!" they might protest. In my estimation, that is a rather insecure position.

A large corporation once brought in a new industrial relations director to help them deal with the continual labor disputes they had been having. The man, who had a long track-record of bringing management and labor together, listened intently through the long briefing he received at his first management meeting.

"We/they, we/they, we/they!" he finally shouted. "It's as if you are trying to set up an adversary relationship!" He reminded the management team that without labor they had no business, and suggested to leaders within the workforce that without management they had no jobs.

To pull the two groups together, he suggested that the factory workers be given a voice in all decisions that affected their work, that managers eat often in the plant's canteens, that executives (including the chairman of the board) punch time cards just like the employees. The workers, in turn, were to assume responsibility for production schedules, quality control, and improving the high absentee rate.

It was a radical departure from past practice, and it took some selling to "both sides," but everyone finally decided to give it a try. Almost instantly, the high absenteeism dropped to a very satisfactory level, production went up, and the quality of the company's products improved substantially.

When both sides of an adversary relationship came together as "the company," disputes dropped off to a minimum. There were several bonuses to the new attitude: first, the work atmosphere improved considerably; second, the turnover rate dropped off sharply; and third, there was more money available for raises. What happened in that situation was that people whose goals seemed vastly different began to identify with each other. Neither side lost its identity. In fact, both "sides" found a new identity in common that both of them wanted.

Do you remember the definition of dialog, from chapter two? "Dialog is what happens when the reality within you, contacts the reality within your audience and, together, you move toward a common new reality." Such dialog can only happen when you and your audience identify with each other—whether your audience is your mate or child, a workforce, or a group of people who have come to hear you speak.

The amateur communicator tends to say, "Let me make my position absolutely clear to you." But the real pros always try to identify with their audiences. When there is an adversary relationship, the pros try to fix the problem, not the blame. Perhaps that is why they can maintain a consistently high audience-response rating.

TYING IT ALL TOGETHER

Your audience-response rating is your effectiveness at getting people to pay attention to you. It will, more than any other factor, determine how successful you are at communicating.

As a communicator, your first and ever-present task is to connect, and maintain connection, with your audience. To do that you must cultivate the audience's sensitivity, awareness, and understanding, and be able to identify with your audience.

In our next chapter, we will look at some of the connecting links—the techniques for making contact with an audience—that the communication pros use. Before you move on, I suggest you take a few minutes to reflect on the strategies I've described, and do the growth exercise below.

GROWTH EXERCISE

What was your most successful attempt recently to communicate with an audience of any size? How did your attitude toward that audience influence each of the following:

1. Were you sensitive to the "presence" of the audience?
2. Were you aware of their feelings, needs, and circumstances?
3. Did you seek to understand that audience?
4. Could you identify with that audience?

It might be helpful to also look at a recent failure in an attempt to communicate, and ask yourself the same questions about the failure. (Of course, I'm assuming that I am not the only one who has ever failed in a communications effort.)

CHAPTER FOUR

HOW TO USE
CONNECTING LINKS

Now you are ready to move on to the next big hurdle in getting people to pay attention to you—getting your audience to identify with you.

If you have mastered the high art of connecting with your audience, it's time to concentrate all your energies on getting your audience to connect with you.

UNDERSTANDING CONNECTING LINKS

Why is it that there are certain people you will listen carefully to, while there are others you simply ignore or even avoid as if they had the plague?

The manager says to the secretary, "screen my calls." What does that order mean? It means simply, "I don't want to spend my time talking to anyone, unless that person has something *important* to say to me!"

You turn on your television set and immediately start flipping the channel selector. You only stop flipping from channel to channel when you find a show you think will be *interesting* to you.

You hear a siren and immediately you begin looking around for the emergency vehicle—especially if you are driving. You want to know if the siren represents a *concern,* or *problem,* to you.

That's what connectors are all about—making your audience

feel that what you have to say is important to them, is interesting to them, or relates significantly to a concern or problem they have. One definition of connect is "to associate in one's mind."

As a communicator, your task is to convince your audience that the time they spend listening to you will be time well invested. That's true whether you are making a speech to a thousand people, or writing a letter to a prospective employer, or attempting to persuade a potential lover to spend an evening with you.

In a world of mass communications, where so many voices are clamoring for attention, your effectiveness as a communicator is directly proportional to your ability to convince your targeted audience that it is you they should choose to spend time listening to. (More will be said about breaking through all the "interference" in later chapters.)

The pros have learned that there are two basic connecting links that enable them to get people to pay attention to them. These are tactics, or ploys, they use to convince an audience that what they have to say will be interesting, or important, or will address significantly a problem or concern of theirs.

The connecting links can only be used effectively when you are sensitive to your audience, when you are aware of your audience, when you understand your audience, and when you identify with your audience. It's this simple: *if you would get your audience to pay attention to you, you must first pay attention to your audience.*

Once you know what your audience wants and needs, you are in position to use one of the connecting links to show them how to get it. Remember, show people what they want and they will move Heaven and earth to get it.

CONNECTING LINK #1: CONNECT THROUGH IMAGES

Do you know the saying, "A picture is worth a thousand words"? We all think in images, or mental pictures.

Go ahead! Check yourself out to see if that statement is really true about you! If you are going to be able to use this connecting link effectively, you need to know how true it really is.

Even if you think in "ideas," you probably process those ideas by images of words or symbols. If I said to you, pick a number between one and ten, you probably would get an image in your mind of the symbol representing the number you have chosen.

Whom would you say was the greatest communicator in all of history? Regardless of the person you chose, I would bet you that person was a master at conveying images.

Jesus spoke in parables, or simple stories, about runaway boys, lost coins, and seeds falling to the ground to connect with His audience of common people. Moses held out the hope of a land "flowing with milk and honey" to encourage a nation of liberated slaves to keep moving toward their goal. When Napoleon's troops were discouraged and dispirited in Egypt, he renewed their commitment to fight by painting word pictures of the scenes of glory that would await them when they returned to France.

Look at the vivid imagery Winston Churchill used during World War II to call forth patriotism in the people of England to rise up and defend their homeland against Adolph Hitler's invading forces. He said, "We shall not flag or fail. We shall fight . . . on the seas and oceans, we shall fight with growing confidence in the air, we shall defend our island, whatever the cost may be, we shall fight on the beaches, we shall fight on the landing grounds, we shall fight in the fields and in the streets, we shall fight in the hills; we shall never surrender." As you read that excerpt from a speech he made before Parliament, you can almost see the valiant soldiers, sailors, and pilots defending their country.

By concentrating on images, a speaker can convince his audience that what he is saying is important, interesting and relevant to their needs and concerns.

Connecting through images involves four basic steps: seeing images clearly, choosing the most effective images, conveying images accurately, and assisting your audience in seeing images. Let's look a little closer at each of the steps.

Step # 1:
See Images Clearly

If your audience is to connect with the image you seek to convey, that image must first be clear to you. If you see the image inaccurately, or if your understanding of that image is fuzzy in your own mind, what you convey to your audience will be inaccurate or fuzzy.

Two of the most useful powers you possess as a communicator are your powers to listen and observe. Someone once said that God gave us two ears, two eyes, and only one mouth: it is clear He meant for us to listen and observe at least twice as much as we speak.

Haven't you known a few people who do a lot more listening and observing than they do talking? They might not say much, but what they say has weight, it has substance, it has clarity. And since what they say is usually interesting, important, and relevant to your needs and concerns, you usually pay attention to it.

Now, did you notice that I did not use the verbs "hearing" and "looking"? I've used "listening" and "observing"—and there is a world of difference.

Hearing is the auditory response of the physical mechanisms we call our ears. It's something we do passively, automatically, and with little effort. We hear the noises of traffic, of a busy workplace, of nature. In fact, we may even go to great lengths to eliminate the noises that bombard our ears with unwanted sounds. We look for a quiet place, or a quiet time in which we can block out the unwanted sounds of our environment. We do this because we want to concentrate on what is important and interesting to us. In other words, we do it because we want to *listen.* We want to tune out all the distractions so we can select those sounds we want to hear.

That's what listening is all about: tuning in on those sounds that matter to us. It involves actively focusing our attention on the sounds we select; it involves thinking and becoming aware of the chosen sounds.

Your ability to convey images accurately and interestingly will be directly related to your ability to listen.

Likewise, looking is the physical response of our eyes to the objects around us. Even as you read this, there are many objects in your environment that could distract you by leading your eyes away from the page. When we *observe* something, we not only focus our eyes upon it, we get involved with it through thinking about it, perhaps even feeling it. Observing is an active pursuit that occurs when we pay attention to something.

Notice sometime how television directors use the camera to direct your attention to a certain person or object. The camera will often "pan" across a room filled with people to set a location and mood. But the directors know that there is a limit to what your eyes can connect with, so they zero in on the one person they want you to observe very closely. They might even focus on one hand of a person to call attention to the action that is about to take place.

Whether we realize it or not, we do the same thing constantly as we select what we will observe. Unfortunately, many people who would be effective communicators become so active at "panning" that they fail to develop their powers to focus on the specific images they would seek to convey. They might look at an object, but they fail to really *observe* that object. Thus, when they seek to describe the object as an image for their audience, the mental picture they convey is so vague or inaccurate that it creates an incomplete or inaccurate picture in the minds of those who are listening.

The real pros at communicating have learned that they can no more create an image of something they have not truly observed than they can come back from a place they have not been. So they learn to concentrate, to pay attention, to become involved with the images they would seek to convey.

If you would become an effective communicator, you must first become a careful observer and listener. As you learn how to focus clearly images in your own mind, you will be able to move on toward conveying those images to the minds of other people.

At the end of this chapter, you will find some growth exercises that can help you develop your skills at listening and observing. If you really want to become an effective communicator, I would suggest that you take advantage of this opportunity to sharpen your skills at listening and observing.

Step #2: Choose Images Carefully

Just as the director of a movie or television show chooses the images that will convey the action and emotion that enables you to follow the storyline, you as a communicator can choose the images that you will use to convey your messages. Of course, that sounds so obvious you might tend to overlook just how important it is. *Your ability to communicate is directly related to your choices of images you will use to convey your messages and meanings.*

Some of the most effective public speakers and writers I know spend more time developing the images they will convey than they do the messages and meanings they want to get across. Usually, they know what they want to say, so they concentrate on the most effective ways to say those things.

Here are some guidelines the experts use in choosing which images they utilize to convey their messages:

1. CHOOSE IMAGES THAT ARE CLEAR AND UNDERSTANDABLE TO YOUR AUDIENCE.   If you suddenly found yourself stranded on a small island and surrounded by cannibals, it is doubtful you would try to use symbols they did not understand to communicate with them. It is more likely that you would try to choose images they would understand to try to convince them that they should not make a pot roast out of you.

Of course, not all efforts at conveying images are that critical, but, to those who would become effective communicators, they are very important. The only way to take advantage of every opportunity to communicate is to choose images that are clear, images that your audience understands.

That's why it is so crucial to know your audience. An image that seems quite clear to you might be very confusing to your audience. And, since you must rely primarily on words to convey that image, the need for clarity is even more crucial.

One of the difficulties I had in learning to communicate with American audiences is that one word in English might have several different meanings. For example, the word "post" can be used to describe: a pole in the ground, a letter, an office where a letter is mailed, a brand of cereal, the process of recording figures in a journal, the displaying of a public notice, informing someone, the stationing of a soldier or guard, a person's position with a company, placing a sign to keep trespassers off a piece of property—and a whole lot more. When I was speaking and used the word post, I could see an image in my mind of what I was talking about. But often my audience was seeing an image that was totally different. I soon learned that if I was going to become an effective communicator I had to choose images that were clear—not only to me, but to my audience as well. As I came to know my audiences and to understand the images that were clear to them, it became easier to connect with them and to get them to connect with me.

Remember: to make images work for—not against—you, always choose images that are clear and understandable to your audience.

2. CHOOSE IMAGES THAT YOUR AUDIENCE CAN IDENTIFY WITH. In pre-television days, some of the most popular radio shows were the "soap operas." Soap operas got their name from the fact that they were serialized programs sponsored by soap companies. The soap companies found them a suitable platform for advertising because millions of women listened to them faithfully every day— and women bought soap.

When television made its debut, network executives automatically assumed that the new medium was a natural for soap operas. So they spent millions of dollars on elaborate sets, hired top-flight actors, and began broadcasting visual versions of the stories women had come to love.

There was only one thing wrong with the theory—it didn't work! The ratings showed that women would watch one or two episodes, then drop out.

Expensive studies were done to determine why women would listen to soap operas on radio, but would not watch them on television. After years of research, and the loss of millions of dollars, the networks finally discovered the problem. A woman in a housecoat, with her hair in curlers, living in a shabby apartment simply couldn't identify with an actress who was thirty pounds lighter, meticulously coiffured, and lived in a mansion. On radio, the stars could look any way the audience chose for them to look.

Not to be outdone, the networks went back to the drawing boards and came up with shows that women identified with. They developed less elaborate sets, hired less glamorous actors, chose storylines that were more like the everyday lives of their audiences. Soon the television soap operas were off and running—quite profitably so. Probably no one in our society has understood—nor cashed in as effectively on—identification as have the programmers of soap operas.

As a communicator, you can convey your messages and meaning much more effectively by choosing images with which your audience can readily identify.

3. CHOOSE IMAGES THAT ARE USEFUL. The after-dinner speaker who tells an opening story just because audiences laugh at it is

wasting a golden opportunity to convey an image that gets the talk off to a productive start.

Of course, if your sole purpose is to entertain your audience, telling one unrelated story after another and creating images that serve no purpose but to get laughs might be a good tactic. However, most of us have more specific goals for our communications efforts than that. Since most of us are competing with many voices that clamor for the attention of our audiences, it is important to make every image we convey a useful image.

When Franklin D. Roosevelt took the reins as President of the United States in 1933, this nation was in the grasp of a great depression. Roosevelt knew that his first task was to inspire confidence in the American economic system. As a master communicator, he took advantage of his first inaugural address to create images of a nation struggling against a common enemy. "The only thing we have to fear is fear itself," he told the masses of people who were hanging on his every word.

Regardless of how we relate to him politically, we have to admit that Roosevelt was a very effective conveyor of images that were useful in presenting his ideas and creating hope. His famous "fireside chats" were very useful in keeping his countrymen abreast of how his administration was handling the task of winning World War II. The quiet and calm tone of voice, the fire softly crackling in the background, and the constant painting of word pictures enabled him to calm the fears and inspire the courage of millions of people.

As you seek to communicate with your audience, remember that the images you choose for that task should all be useful—they should convey exactly what you wish them to convey.

4. CHOOSE IMAGES THAT ARE VIVID.   The more vivid an image is, the better it attracts the attention of your audience and the more it conveys.

William Shakespeare's plays literally come alive with vivid images that convey his meanings, moods, and messages. Consider, for example, the aftermath of the fight scene from "Romeo and Juliet." Romeo's friend, who has been stabbed with a sword, is told that the wound is only superficial. He protests: "No, 'tis not so deep as a well, nor so wide as a church door; but 'tis enough, 'twill serve: ask for me tomorrow, and you shall find me a grave man." With that vivid imagery, the skilled dramatist sets up his audience for the ensuing death and the massive conflict which follows it. No amount of words could have created the mood as effectively as Shakespeare's vivid image.

Notice sometime how a skilled speaker uses images that come alive with meaning. That speaker knows that lively and well-chosen images can convey much more than words alone could ever convey.

To become effective as a conveyor of images, choose those images that vividly call attention to your message or meaning.

5. CHOOSE IMAGES THAT ARE CONCISE.   An image that is concise enough to speak for itself can be a great aid in communicating a complicated message.

Many people have sought to describe the awesome fence that Russia erected along the European border shortly after World War II. It has been called the "Berlin Wall," "The Great Wall," and many other names. However, none of its names conveys the image of the wall so effectively as the name given to it by Sir Winston Churchill. He called it "The Iron Curtain."

To get a clear picture of just how valuable concise images can be to the communicator, I suggest you study the way they are used by the producers of television commercials. Look, for example, at how much meaning is conveyed by slogans like "Reach out and touch someone," or "When you care enough to send the very best." The commercial makers know that they have less than thirty seconds to get their messages across, so they pack those spots with clear, concise images that tell their stories simply and powerfully.

In almost any form of communication, brevity is a major secret of success. And nothing aids brevity like the use of concise images.

6. CHOOSE IMAGES THAT ARE MEMORABLE.   As a communicator, you not only want people to pay attention to what you say, you want them to remember it. People remember images much more easily than they remember words.

"One small step for a man, one giant leap for mankind" was the image flashed back to the earth after the first step was taken on the moon. To be sure, we remember the occasion; but the image created by the words helps a great deal in making the occasion so memorable.

Think of some of the great speeches you remember and very likely it is the images used by the speakers that you find so memorable. For example, you probably recall Dr. Martin Luther King's famous "I Have A Dream" speech, with its imagery of "little black children and little white children playing together on the red hills of Georgia."

Great communicators have a way of choosing images that people will remember for years to come. Likewise, all effective communicators leave you with images that will assist you in remembering what they have said.

Step #3: Convey Images Accurately

Images are valuable aids in communicating, but only if they are conveyed accurately. After you have clearly seen an image in your own mind and chosen that image as the most effective way of getting your message across, you must put it into words that create the same image in the minds of those who hear you.

Now, that might sound simple, but it isn't. In fact, accurately conveying images is one of the toughest challenges you face as a communicator. The image you describe and the image your audience sees in their own minds, might be significantly different. When that happens, the image becomes a hindrance to communicating instead of an aid. It's like the Sunday school teacher who quoted a passage from Proverbs that says, "The wicked flee when no man pursueth." He sought to convey that "ungodly" people are nervous, even when there is no danger of their being caught. But one of his pupils heard him say "The wicked flea," and immediately thought of an evil insect running from the exterminator.

The problem stems from the fact that the images we seek to convey don't stand alone in the minds of our audiences. They are fitted into the collection of other images that are already in the minds of the people who hear us.

To get a clear picture of how much this problem afflicts communicators, think about some of the difficulties created when idiomatic expressions used by statesmen are translated into other languages. Nikita Khrushchev apparently was trying to express his belief in the superiority of the communist economic system over the private enterprise system when he made his famous "inflammatory" speech at the United Nations. His message was translated as "We will bury you!" What. Mr. Khrushchev sought to convey was not at all what his audience heard, and the result was a serious misunderstanding between two nations that took a lot of diplomatic maneuvering to overcome. Not all mis-conveyed images are as explosive, nor do they carry with them the serious consequences of that famous slip; but they can significantly hinder all of us who would be effective communicators.

It is a good idea always to ask yourself two questions before you try to convey an image to an audience: first, how might this audience misinterpret the image I seek to convey? and, second, how can I avoid the misinterpretation? Remember, it is not so much what you say to an audience that counts: it is what that audience hears you say that registers.

Speakers and writers must depend on words to convey their images and, as we have already seen, words can be very confusing. Words can have several widely different meanings; they can have different shades of meanings to different audiences; and they can be mistaken by those who hear them because they sound like other words.

To add to the confusion, words often change in meaning over a period of time. Take, for example, the word "cool." Once it meant only a degree of temperature. Later, it evolved to mean "detached" or "aloof." Now, in some circles, it means "aware," or "self-contained."

Since all images must be reduced to words, and words can be confusing, the task of the speaker or writer is to make sure that the words accurately convey the image to the audience, and enable that audience to attach the meaning intended to that image.

Step #4: Assist Your Audience
in Interpreting Images

The effort to convey an image is not complete until that image is reformed in the minds of the audience.

A skilled communicator is never satisfied to say, "you misunderstood what I said." The pros know that it is their task to make sure their messages are received accurately and with the weight they want them to have. Remember, the goal of effective communication is "to obtain a desired response." The task of the communicator is not complete until that response is achieved. Therefore, you must not only see images clearly, choose carefully what images you will convey, and convey those images accurately; you must also assist your audience in reformulating the images in their own minds.

To help you do that, there are four very useful tools: repetition, reinforcement, feedback, and application. Let's look at each of them.

TOOL #1: REPETITION.   Few people can repeat what they have heard said only a short time before. An hour later, even fewer can accurately repeat what they have heard. Some experts say we remember less than one-third of what we hear for twenty-four hours or longer. The percentage of what we retain, however, goes up markedly when we hear it repeated several times.

Thus, skilled communicators help their audiences to capture and interpret images by repeating the most significant images— again and again—until they are sure their audiences will remember them. I'm aware that this goes against what most of us learned in school. There, we were taught that a good speaker never repeats what has been said because it will bore the audience. But I have found that the opposite is true. Generally, an audience will appreciate a restatement of images because it helps them to remember them.

There are several useful devices that can help you repeat what you've said without sounding like a broken record.

You can restate or review what you have just said. The phrase, "in other words," indicates that you are repeating a message in a different way so the audience can get a clearer view of the image. If your audience does not understand what you have said, it will help them focus it more clearly. If they do understand, it will help them remember it.

Next, you can summarize what you have just said. By succinctly repeating significant points, you enable the audience to remember them.

And you can interpret what you have said. "If it is true that . . . it means that . . ." is a strong way of reinforcing through repetition.

Also, you can call attention to special things that should be remembered. It is often helpful to simply say, "remember this . . . ," and restate what you have said.

P. T. Barnum, the great circus promoter, had a philosophy that many expert communicators find useful. "Tell 'em what you're goin' to tell 'em, then tell 'em, and then tell 'em what you've told 'em," he often said in instructing the "front men" whom he sent ahead of the circus to generate excitement and swell attendance. It's not a bad approach to helping an audience reformulate images in their own minds.

TOOL #2: REINFORCEMENT.   It is often very helpful to prop up an image with other images so that people can get it fixed clearly in their minds. This can be done very effectively through several different approaches.

Visual reinforcement can be provided by the use of slides or transparencies, objects that are held up for attention, and by giving your audience handout sheets with the significant images printed on them. It has been proven that people remember, and understand more precisely, what they see than what they simply hear.

Verbal reinforcement can be given by painting other word pictures that emphasize the image you wish to convey. For example, during a talk I will often say, "Now, when I told that to an audience in [another city], they. . . ." Then I recreate the image as I described it to that other audience, and describe their reaction to it.

Supportive data can also be used effectively to reinforce an image you wish your audience to re-create in their minds. Someone once said, "The strongest influence is raw information." If the image is important to the message you wish to convey, support that image with additional information that will aid the audience in fixing it clearly in their minds. You might preface the data with a remark like, "In case you question what I have just said, look at the results of this study. . . ." Another technique, and one that has been used often by reporters on television documentaries, is to simply give several pieces of information to support a claim under the title of "Item."

TOOL #3: FEEDBACK.   To make sure that your audience understands your images clearly, ask them to repeat back to you what you have said, or to interpret for you what it means to them.

Sometimes this approach can be rather disconcerting—especially if the audience has not caught your image at all. In a later chapter I will talk much more about how the prejudices and biases of an audience can cause them to completely miss, or misinterpret images you thought you had conveyed very clearly. Those of us who spend our lives as professional communicators know that audiences sometimes hear us say precisely the opposite of what we mean.

However, as painful as it may at times be, getting a clear picture of what your audience has seen in the image you used is the only way to correct wrong impressions. Too often, those who would communicate look to feedback as a way of getting compliments for a good piece of writing or a speech. To do that is to miss the real value of what feedback can do for you. Since your goal is to get a desired response, your top priority should be to find out which misconceptions are present so that you can deal with them.

Some years ago, I was called in by a Midwest corporation that had annual sales volume of about $13 million. They were concerned about their stagnant growth rate, and felt it was related to poor performance by many of their employees. As a consultant, I was asked to study the problem and make recommendations for improvement.

Upon looking into the company's communications systems, I discovered that what went out from the home office as "crystal clear" memos and directives were often misinterpreted by people in the field. Likewise, letters to the home office were often misunderstood. As a result, many people within the company felt insecure, were confused as to what they should be doing, and were afraid they were going to lose their jobs.

My suggestion to them was that we hold several seminars throughout the company on how to communicate effectively. At first, the idea seemed like a waste of effort—at least from the company's point of view. Top management felt they were doing a good job of communicating because people often complimented them on their speeches and other communications. But, reluctantly, they agreed to give it a try.

As a result, management was able to correct some erroneous impressions: employees came to understand the wishes and instructions of management, and the whole organization came together as a team. When people at all levels within the company began to clear up all the misconceptions and missed signals, they found they could work together, and actually enjoyed being a part of a winning team. (The company's performance improved so much that it was later sold to another major corporation for $24 million.)

The secret to obtaining feedback is not in asking, "Do you understand what I said?" but in asking, "What did you understand me to say?" It is only when you know what people have understood from the images you have sought to convey that you can clarify incorrect interpretations of your images and their meanings.

TOOL #4: APPLICATION.   Perhaps the most effective method of assisting an audience in reformulating your images in their mind is application.

"What I hear, I forget; what I see, I may remember; but what I do, I understand," is an old saying. The implication is clear: if you would have your audience understand the image you wish to convey and the message behind it, let them do something that will make it a part of their own experience.

To help you see how this works, let me suggest that you do the following exercise, which I often use to illustrate the importance of following directions correctly. (I have altered it slightly to use it in this book.) To complete the test you will need a blank sheet of paper.

CAN YOU FOLLOW DIRECTIONS?

(This is a timed test—allow yourself only three minutes to complete)

1. Read everything *before you do anything.*
2. Print your name in the upper right corner of the paper.
3. Write the word "name" under your name.
4. Draw five squares in the upper left corner of the paper.
5. Put an "X" in each of the squares.
6. Put a circle around each of the squares.
7. Sign your name in the lower left corner of the paper.
8. Write "yes, yes, yes," after your signature.
9. Draw a circle around your signature and the words "yes, yes, yes."
10. Put a large "S" in the lower right corner of the paper.
11. Draw a triangle around the "S".
12. In the center of the paper multiply 703 by 66.

13. Draw a rectangle around your answer.
14. If you have carefully followed my directions, write "I have" in the top center of the paper.
15. Now that you have finished reading everything, do only as I directed in the first sentence. Place the blank sheet back in its package and continue reading the book.

In seminars where I use this quiz, I include several instructions that tell participants to say certain things aloud. It is always interesting to see how many of them do not read everything—as they were instructed to do in the first sentence—before they do anything. By allowing people to experience their tendency not to follow directions correctly, I enable them to see the point much more clearly than I could by simply telling them that most people don't follow directions carefully. It's always an amusing exercise; but more than that, it helps people to see things clearly by letting them apply it to themselves.

CONNECTING LINK #2:
CONNECT THROUGH STORIES

A good story is to a speech or piece of writing what a window is to a house—it lets in the light. The real pros in communicating know that, and use stories often and well.

But stories can only help you connect with your audience when they are carefully chosen, skilfully told, and artfully applied to what you are saying. Everything I said about images in the preceding section can be applied to stories, but there are some special considerations to keep in mind when using verbal illustrations. In this section we will look at a few of them.

FEW PEOPLE USE STORIES WELL.   As a professional speaker, I have had the opportunity of sharing the platform with some of the best-known individuals in the world. Often, I have been very disappointed at their speeches because, while they were obviously brilliant and eminently qualified to speak on a subject, they failed to help me—and the rest of the audience—to connect with what they were saying.

Conversely, I have shared the platform with some of the most outstanding speakers in the world—people who had become the top names in the speaking profession simply because of their skills at communicating with audiences.

What makes the difference? Why is it that an outstanding business executive, or a world-famous authority on a subject, or a beloved statesman will often leave an audience cold and disappointed, while a skilled communicator will bring that same audience to its feet in uproarious applause?

More often than not, I have noticed that the difference is in the frequency with which the speakers use stories. For example, I once watched Dr. Norman Vincent Peale make a sleepy audience at a convention in New Orleans, where we were both speaking, literally come alive. He made them laugh and he made them cry, he entertained them and informed them, and he challenged them and inspired them—and he did it with his marvelous skills as a storyteller. He told funny stories and he told sad stories, he told stories of failures and he told stories of successes, and he illustrated every point he made with a strong story. Believe me, he was a hard act to follow.

Even more impressive to me is the fact that even now—many years later—I can remember much of what he said, and many of the stories he told.

LEARN HOW TO USE STORIES—INCREASE YOUR IMPACT. If you would increase your effectiveness as a communicator, if you would increase your audience-response rating, learn how to use stories well and use them often.

"I don't have time to tell stories," one of America's foremost business leaders once told me. "I only have about twenty minutes to make the speech." (He had asked me to look over his speech and give him some pointers on presenting it.)

"Sir," I replied, "you don't have time *not* to tell stories!"

"What do you mean?" he asked.

"You need to connect quickly with your audience, you need to help them understand precisely what you have to say, and you need for them to act on what you are telling them," I replied. "Nothing can accomplish those goals as effectively as a few well-placed stories."

"But they will listen to me because of who I am," he protested. "And they will do what I tell them because I'm the boss."

"It is a mistake for even the President of the United States to make those assumptions," I pointed out. Then I reminded him that even Abraham Lincoln opened his most famous speech—the Gettysburg Address—with a story of a nation caught in a struggle for its own identity and survival. I used a story to tell him the importance of using stories.

"I see what you mean," he replied.

Together, we went through his speech, cutting out explanations and adding stories. His audience loved it, and he later told me it was the most effective speech he had ever given.

"You've made a confirmed storyteller out of me," he said.

I hope to do the same for you.

Tip # 1: Choose Stories Carefully

Like images, stories must be chosen carefully if they are to act as illustrations for the points you want to get across. Here are some of the criteria I use in selecting stories:

First, it must be a story to which my audience can readily relate. It might be about a common experience we have all shared, a fear or concern we all share, an interest we hold in common, or a problem we all face. My primary concern is that there not be one person in that audience who couldn't relate readily to the story I choose.

For example, I once spoke at the annual sales meeting of Borden's, Inc., which was held in Houston. Immediately upon receiving the invitation, I began to think about all the great stories I'd heard about "Elsie the Cow." However, as I always do, I checked with someone within the company to find out if that was a suitable subject.

"Heavens no!" shouted my contact. "We consider Elsie almost sacred!"

By checking to make sure that the stories I planned to use were appropriate and were stories that audience could relate to, I saved myself some embarrassment and was able to use other stories that my audience could connect with.

Second, the story must be clear and stand on its own. A story that is confusing, or has to be explained to an audience, serves as a hindrance rather than an aid.

Have you ever told a joke that went over like a lead balloon because no one understood the punchline? It's a mistake that even some of the top pros make occasionally. A joke, or a story, might seem perfectly clear to them, but when they tell it, the audience just stares at them blankly. I learned a little trick a long time ago that helps me keep that problem to a bare minimum. I always practice telling every story to several different people before I try it on an audience. That way, I can weed out the stories that don't communicate what I want to say.

Third, the story must relate clearly the point I wish to make. It is not enough that the story be poignant or funny; it must carry its weight in adding clarity to what I am saying. After you have told a story, the audience should have no question as to how it fits in with the theme of your message, nor which is the particular point you are emphasizing with it.

Fourth, the story must be one I can tell well. Some stories are very funny when they are told by one person, but fall flat when they are told by another. Likewise, some stories pack a real emotional wallop when told by one person, but lose all their impact when someone else tells them. A story must be suited to the personality of the teller, and must fit in with the mood of the speech or piece of writing.

Finally, the story must be usable in the allotted time. If you are building up to a major point, you might want to stretch your story out to obtain full emotional impact. But if you are illustrating a relatively minor point, you will want to tell the story in a very short time.

Now, some stories don't deserve stretching, and others can't be told well in a few words. It is a good idea to choose only stories that can be told within the length of time you think they deserve.

Tip #2: Practice Telling a Story

Many amateurs spend hours and hours writing out their main points and practicing the delivery of strong points they want to make. Yet, they simply assume they can tell every story in their talk without practicing it. If a story is important enough to tell, it is important enough to deserve practice. A good story has a rhythm, a mood, a flow to it. You can only pick up those things when you tell the story over and over until it is a part of you.

Tip #3: Let Your Audience React

ABC commentator Paul Harvey has remained the top-rated radio personality in America for many years, and is widely sought as a public speaker. One reason he attracts such large audiences is that he is a master at using the pause for maximum effect. He pauses to allow the audience to anticipate what his punchline will be, and then pauses to allow the line to sink in completely before moving on to his next statement. As a result, people hang on his every word.

A big part of telling stories successfully is letting the audience digest those stories as you go along, and allowing the punchlines to sink in when they are finished. Skillful storytellers tell stories like conductors play symphonies.

Tip #4: Involve Your Audience

Most audiences love stories and will become quite involved in them if you give them the opportunity. There are several ways you can do that.

As you tell a story, you can ask questions that lead the audience along with you. For example, I often use questions like, "What do you think he did after that?" If the audience is really with me, they will shout back the answer.

The best way I've found to involve the audience in funny stories is to tell the stories as if they were about people in the audience. The results can often be hilarious and very effective in conveying messages. The technique works on the same principles as do the "roastings" that have become so popular in recent years. By good-naturedly picking on a big executive, or a member of the group who is always clowning, or even a highly respected individual, you can connect with that audience and very effectively set up a point you want to make.

There are three important cautions about using this technique. First, always make sure you clear it with the person before you start giving him or her a "mini-roast." At least make sure you check with someone who knows the person in order to be certain the "guinea pig" has enough of a sense of humor that he or she will not be easily offended. Secondly, keep it good-natured. Most audiences resent an outsider coming in and "attacking" a member of their group. And, finally, keep it short. A dragged out story about a member of the audience tends to become boring, and the protracted attention can become embarrassing to the individual involved.

Tip #5: Apply the Story

Sometimes, even the most alert audiences will not get the point you are attempting to reinforce with a story. After you have given an audience a chance to react to the story, it is always a good idea to state briefly the point you are trying to get across. (You can do this with a statement like, "So you see. . . .")

When you apply the story to the point you are making, you not only make sure the audience gets the point, you reinforce the point through repetition.

TYING IT ALL TOGETHER

The two most effective ways of getting an audience to connect with you and to identify with what you are saying are to use images and use stories.

Images help people to see clearly what you have to say, they enable people to associate what you are saying with what they already know or feel, and they help them remember what you have said long after your talk.

Illustrative stories are like windows—they let in the light. You can use stories to enable your audience to connect with what you have to say—but only when your stories are carefully chosen, skilfully told, and artfully applied.

GROWTH EXERCISES

EXERCISE #1: PRACTICE OBSERVING IMAGES.   Take off your wrist watch and, without looking at it, place it where you cannot see it. Now, pretend that you are describing that watch to a person on the other end of a telephone line. Make a list of at least twenty components that go into making up the over-all image of that watch. Describe the face, the case, the band, the hands or digits—every detail.

Now take out the watch and see how accurate your description is. You might be surprised at how many details you failed to list, and how many you described incorrectly.

For further growth, do this exercise with several different, but common, objects such as a coffee cup, a desk calender, and a lamp.

EXERCISE #2: PRACTICE LISTENING TO DESCRIPTIONS.   Listen carefully to a news item on a radio newscast. Turn off the radio and attempt to recreate the story as accurately as you can. See how many details you can recall, including names, locations, times, dates, ages, descriptions of people and places, etc. If the newscast is repeated at a later time, check your list against the details as you hear them again.

For further growth, practice listening to an entire five-minute newscast and listing all of the stories in the order in which they were told.

EXERCISE #3: PRACTICE TELLING A STORY.   Tell a story, just as if you were in front of an audience, into a cassette recorder. Do as good a job as you can at telling the story. Then play it back several times and evaluate your own rendition as if you were a member of an audience made up of people you don't know. Write down ways you might improve in future tellings.

For further growth, do this exercise with several stories. Keep practicing them until you feel comfortable in telling them.

CHAPTER FIVE

COPING WITH INTERFERENCE

You write a letter that you are sure will get results—and nothing happens.

Or you stand to speak to an audience with a message you feel is highly important, and the audience fidgets restlessly until you finish; they never listen to a word you say.

Or perhaps you give a set of detailed instructions to an individual only to have that person stare blankly at you and say, "Excuse me, what did you say?"

In each of these instances, you've got "static" or "interference" on the line of communication between you and your audience. It's a little like driving past the broadcast antenna of a radio station while listening to another station. As soon as you come into the range of the antenna, the signal from that station overrides the signal you're tuned to, and the two stations fight to be heard. Until the interference is eliminated, you might as well forget listening to the station you had previously chosen.

ALL COMMUNICATORS FACE INTERFERENCE

Peter Drucker, often called the "father of American Management," claims that sixty percent of all management problems are a result of faulty communications. A leading marriage counselor says that at least half of all divorces result from faulty communications between spouses. And criminologists tell us that upwards of ninety percent of all criminals have difficulty communicating with other people.

What's the problem? Is it lack of communication? Certainly not!

With the instant and mass communications systems that now exist, this is the most "connected" generation in history. If anything, we over-communicate. We send signals at an overwhelming pace. It's now possible to pick up more than 100 television channels on a receiver; a sensitive radio receiver can tune in more than 100 stations; and more magazines, books and newspapers are published now than ever before. It seems there is always someone shouting to be heard.

Any person who attempts to communicate with another, or to any group, can expect to encounter resistance, or "interference." Why? Because there are just too many voices clamoring to be heard. People have to select the voices they listen to, because it is impossible to tune in to all of them. If you want to send messages like the pros do, you must find ways of breaking through all of that interference. (Remember, the communications cycle is not complete until your audience has heard your message and given the response you desire.)

In this chapter, we will focus on how to identify interference, how to pin down its source, and how to cope with it.

WHAT IS INTERFERENCE?

I define interference as any obstacle preventing a message reaching its intended audience with the desired impact. It might be helpful to think of interference as a barrier, or a wall, that stands between you and a person, or persons, with whom you wish to connect.

Most barriers to communication can be divided into one of two categories: competition and resistance. The messages you wish to send are either competing with your messages, or resisted by those you wish to receive them. In either case, you must penetrate the barrier or face the fact that your message will not be received.

More than anything else, it is your attitude toward those barriers that will determine how successful you will be in getting your message across. The amateur is often satisfied to say, "They just won't listen to me!" but the professional attitude is, "It is up to me to find a way to crash through the barriers and make sure my message is heard!"

Of course, there are times when even the professionals cannot break through all the barriers. Once I was invited to speak at a beautiful resort hotel in Hilton Head, South Carolina. Now, usually, I love resort settings because they tend to help people relax and become receptive to what I wish to say. But this time the mood was too relaxed. When I arrived, I noticed that a cocktail party was in progress. It had started about 3:00 P.M. and lasted through the dinner hour. By the time I was introduced to speak, the audience was drunk, the waiters were still taking orders for drinks, and people were throwing bread from one table to another. It became obvious very quickly that no meaningful communication could take place between me and that audience. Experiences like this have caused most professional speakers simply to decline invitations to speak at conventions where they are scheduled immediately following cocktail hours.

Sometimes the most productive thing you can do is to avoid an attempt to communicate unless you can overcome the competition and resistance. Remember, communicating is "the right person, saying the right thing, to the right people, at the right place, at the right time, in the right way." It is a frustrating waste of time and energy to try to penetrate barriers that cannot be penetrated.

UNDERSTAND THE LIMITS OF COMMUNICATION

A parent attempting to say the right words to make a "grounded" teenager feel good about it is wasting time, and is often making the youngster feel worse. No amount of wordage can take away the sting of lost privileges. Likewise, looking for a few words that will make the hurt go away after a friend has lost a loved one is a hopeless search. Some words might bring comfort, but it takes more than even the most beautiful words to heal the pain of loss. An employer cannot wipe away the anxiety of an employee who has just been laid-off by giving that person a "pep-talk," nor can a jilted lover quickly respond to an invitation to "find someone else."

There are definite limits to what you can accomplish with words.

Certain circumstances also limit what you can do with communications. For example, some messages are too complex to convey within a few minutes. Others are too complex for an audience to grasp, at least under the existing circumstances. Still others are too complex for the speaker or writer to convey.

Another limitation of communication is that there are certain messages that cannot be received from a particular person because of the nature of the relationship between the sender and the receiver. For example, a black minister might find it an impossible challenge to address a Ku Klux Klan rally on the subject of racial prejudice.

The effective communicator understands that there are limits to what can be done with communications and seeks to work within those limitations. I have turned down many attractive speaking invitations because I knew that I was not the right speaker for a certain audience or set of circumstances. By avoiding the situations in which the barriers are insurmountable, you can concentrate on messages to audiences that can receive them.

TAILOR THE MESSAGE AND PRESENTATION

A minister calling in on a grieving person who has just lost a loved one might be very comforting simply by placing a hand on the shoulder of the bereaved and saying, "I know it hurts, and I care." A gentle touch and a few well-chosen words might communicate much more than a long lecture on how the person must keep on going.

In a similar fashion, it might be much more productive for a speaker to choose a simple topic than to attempt to boil down a three-day seminar into a message that can be given in five minutes. And since people seldom read long letters, it is usually more productive to write a short letter than a long one and, if necessary, enclose supportive documents and explanatory sheets.

(Much more will be said in a later chapter on the subject of tailoring your message and presentation to minimize the effects of interference.)

IDENTIFY THE SOURCE OF BARRIERS

Some would-be communicators seem oblivious to interference. They just plod on with their talking or writing as if their audience was excitedly receiving every word they had to say.

A friend of mine, who operated a storefront recreation center for teenagers, told me of a speaker who visited the center and asked to show some slides she had taken for a community beautification project. Thinking some of the young people might become interested, he agreed to let her show the slides and give her presentation. The room was very dark, and the woman droned on and on about each slide, while her audience of about fifty youngsters silently slipped out the back door. By the end of her hour-and-forty-five-minute presentation, there was only one person left in the audience—and he was asleep.

Obviously, the communicator can create barriers that make it impossible to communicate, but here we're talking more about barriers that exist within the environment or originate with the audience.

Environmental barriers, such as distractions, disturbances, interruptions, and audience discomfort, create competition that causes the audience to pay attention to something other than the communicator. The other type of barrier, resistance, has to do with those walls the audience erects because of an emotional or intellectual reluctance to hear what is being said.

The first step in coping with competition or resistance is identifying the interference. There are several ways you can do this. For convenience, we will use examples primarily from public speaking situations—although the principles apply to almost any situation involving communication.

MONITOR THE ENVIRONMENT

Many speaking attempts are doomed before they get started because of factors in the environment that compete with the speaker. The situation I described earlier in which the entire audience was drunk before I started speaking, and was still drinking during my speech, is a prime example of how the environment can close off any hope of communicating effectively.

Professional speakers know that there are certain conditions that are difficult to compete with, and have learned to work closely with meeting planners to try to eliminate them before a session begins.

With respect to the conditions of a communications environment, there are at least five troublespots to deal with.

Troublespot # 1:
An Unsuitable Location

The size, shape, and location of a room can often determine how much competition you will have. When I spoke at the famous Dunes Resort Hotel in Las Vegas, I was faced with tremendous competition because of the size of the room. A room that is too large can create a space barrier between you and your audience which makes eye contact impossible and allows for distractions from other sources. The meeting was held in the ballroom, which had high ceilings and seating for several thousand people. The group that night was about a fourth of the capacity of the room and (as is usually the case) all the members of the audience sat in the back of the room. When I stood to speak, those people seemed to be a half mile away from me. I was headed for a disaster. Fortunately, the hotel was equipped with spotlights and a very long microphone cord, and I was able to move to the audience and walk among them.

On the other hand, a room that is too small can make people uncomfortable and give them a feeling of being packed in. Add the smoke of a few inconsiderate people to a crowded room, and you have competition that is very hard to cope with.

Also, some rooms have very poor acoustics. If you turn down the public address system, the audience can't hear you; turn it up, and the sound echoes around as if you were in a cave.

Some groups like the idea of meeting outside—particularly in a resort setting. The great outdoors is too big for any speaker to compete with, unless he or she is an expert speaking about the environment.

If you have any input on room choice, suggest a room tailored to the size of the group and fitted acoustically to the speaking activity. Before you speak, monitor the environment and make plans to deal with any competition it creates. Simply to ignore the environment is to surrender to the competition.

Troublespot #2: Uncomfortable Temperature or Lighting

The temperature and lighting of a room can either work for you or against you. If you try to speak in a room that is too warm and is dimly lighted—especially immediately after lunch or a "happy hour"—then your audience will become drowsy, listless, and inattentive. If the conditions are very bad, you might even get competition from snores.

On the other hand, a room that is too cool can make an audience restless and inattentive; while too much lighting can destroy the feeling of intimacy you are seeking to create, and can even make your audience tense.

It is always best to check your room temperature and the lighting conditions before you stand up to speak. There are two important reasons I say this. First, when you stand to speak, you will have enough on your mind. Second, as you speak, your activity and excitement will naturally make you warmer than your audience.

Any time you sense that your audience is physically uncomfortable, stop and try to do something about it. Otherwise, you'll lose out to the competition.

Troublespot #3: Faulty Equipment

A balky or inadequate public address system, or a projector that doesn't work properly, can give most of us more competition than we can handle.

Great strides have been made in audio and visual equipment in recent years. However, I speak in some of the finest facilities in the world and I am constantly dismayed at how building managers will spend millions of dollars on an auditorium, and then balk at spending $500 for a public address system. But whether the problem arises from cheap equipment, poor operators, or from circumstances beyond everybody's control, it is a solution you should seek—not someone to blame.

I've always found it a very good idea to arrive early enough to check out beforehand all equipment I will be using and to eliminate any problems I find. Also, I like to talk with the person who will be operating the equipment to make sure he or she understands my needs and wishes.

Troublespot #4: Visual Distractions

I once spoke to a salespeople's convention at a resort hotel, where the meeting room had an open view to the swimming pool. Now, since all the people in the room were men, and the pool was filled with lovely ladies in revealing bathing suits, I found the competition very keen that day.

Often there are distractions within the room itself. Those of us who speak often have found competition from waiters clearing tables or serving food, people getting up and wandering around, other people taking pictures with bright flashes, and many other actions that compete for the attention of the audience.

Again, any visual distractions that can be eliminated in advance should be dealt with as effectively as possible. If distractions occur during the talk, it is usually better to stop until they are dealt with, and then move on.

Troublespot #5: Noises

Unpleasant sounds seem to come from everywhere—and at the times you least want them. I've had competition from jackhammers breaking up concrete, kitchen workers playing or fighting, other meetings or parties, airplanes overhead flying low, as well as other sources far too numerous to name.

Sometimes, the competition comes from sounds that are not unpleasant—in fact, that's the problem. They are so attractive that they draw the audience away from you. The soft music from a Muzak system, or a band in an adjoining room, can be very distracting.

If you want to keep your speech from being drowned out

by distracting noises, you will need to do everything you can to eliminate them, or develop a strategy for out-performing them.

APPLICATION.   Monitoring the environment is the task of any person who wishes to communicate, whether as a public speaker, a conversationalist, writer of books or articles, or a writer of letters. As you approach the task creatively, you will be amazed at how many of the competing distractions you can eliminate. If you cannot eliminate them, you must develop strategies for dealing with them. To simply ignore them is to give up and let the competing voices have your audience.

MONITOR YOUR AUDIENCE

In chapter three I spoke about the importance of being sensitive and aware of your audience at all times. This is particularly important in the matter of identifying barriers that block you from communicating with your audience. It is this factor that makes advance preparation and practice of what you are going to say so crucial. If you are composing your talk as you go along, or constantly looking at a text or notes, you will not have the presence of mind to really monitor the audience to see if they are being distracted by competition.

A change in the response level of your audience will often be the first signal you will receive that something is drawing their attention away from you.

OBSERVE YOUR AUDIENCE.   Watch everything your audience does and observe any symptom of wandering attention or difficulty in following you. Look for signs that people in the back of the room are having problems hearing you clearly, pause periodically to see that everyone has a clear view of you and anything you want them to see, and correct the problems before you proceed.

If people who were sitting alertly and maintaining eye contact with you are beginning to slump in their chairs, or their eyes have begun to rove, it often indicates that the room is uncomfortable for some reason. It is always a good idea to pin down the source of the problem before you lose them completely.

Remain sensitive to such problems as people sitting too long in one position, or needing to go to the restroom, or struggling with chairs that are uncomfortable. A stand-up exercise, or even a short break, can often rescue a speech that is giving way to the competition of squirming and shifting restlessly.

MONITOR AUDIENCE RESISTANCE

As a communicator, you will sometimes find that the audience resists what you have to say because of emotional or intellectual factors. Let me illustrate. The Nabisco Company invited me to speak at the annual business meeting of their National Biscuit Division, which was held at Dorado Beach, Puerto Rico. When I walked into the room, I realized that every person there was significantly older than myself. They could have easily resisted me as a "kid" who had nothing of value to say to them. To compensate, I remained hidden at the back of the room until I was introduced to speak. Then I walked briskly to the front of the room, picked up the microphone, and started involving them in some strong exercises. Pretty soon the emotional barrier of age difference came down, and we had a great time together.

I encountered an intellectual barrier in another meeting. The occasion was a big meeting of the Diamond Shamrock Corporation in a resort area of Florida. I did not know until I arrived that there would be people from all over the world in my audience that day. Many of them knew very little English, so I was faced with the challenge of communicating through a language barrier. To break down the barrier, I slowed down my speech and used some stories of how I came to America without understanding the language or customs of the people. By recognizing the problem and coming up with a strategy for dealing with it, I was able to pull the foreign visitors in and further enhance the international flair of the meeting.

Now, had I not been aware of those emotional and intellectual barriers, those two audiences would have at best been only partially receptive to what I had to say. But by recognizing the barriers and dealing with them, I was able to turn both presentations into worthwhile dialog.

Some audience resistance, however, is not so easily dealt with.

A major corporation once asked me to give a strong motivational talk to its sales force. What they didn't tell me was that just before I was to speak they planned to announce a major shake-up in the sales division. As a result, I was greeted by a hostile and confused audience of salespeople who had just had their territories restructured, and in some cases their income reduced. They readily assumed I had teamed up with management against them and threw up strong barriers of resistance.

Those situations are tough to deal with, but they become even worse when you try to pretend they don't exist. If you walk into a situation in which there has been a tragedy involving several members of the audience, it is foolish to stand up and crack one joke after another—particularly jokes that relate to the kind of people or tragedy involved.

Sensitivity is the key to monitoring audience resistance, but here are a couple of techniques that can help you with the monitoring process.

LISTEN TO THE AUDIENCE RESPONSE.   When emotional or intellectual resistance is present, you can spot it immediately by the way the audience responds to your one-liners and stories. Audience response is to the public speaker what symptoms are to a doctor. The sensitive speaker knows what kind of response to expect and, when that response is not forthcoming, he or she seeks to determine why.

CONSTANTLY CHECK YOUR AUDIENCE-RESPONSE RATING.   Many professional speakers find it helpful to test the waters periodically to see if the audience is resisting or receiving the messages they are sending. They not only want to know if the audience is backing away from them, they want to know if the audience is grasping the messages they are trying to get across. This can be done with such ploys as asking a question that the audience can answer with one word. If the audience shouts back the answer, you know you're getting through. If only a few people respond, it is a good idea to check further to see if you are losing most of your audience.

Remember, the effective communicator knows what response is desired and constantly checks to see that the desired response is building up throughout the whole talk.

"What's the last thing you did in your sermon?" the professor asked the ministerial student who had just delivered his first sermon.

"I woke up my audience," came the sad reply.

Most of us are not that bad, but we could become a lot better at getting people to pay attention to us and to what we have to say. It takes more than a good speech on a vital subject by a qualified speaker to really connect with an audience. Remember, to be an effective communicator you must say what you have to say in the right way, it must be heard and received by your audience, and it must produce the response you desire.

Think about some of the speakers you have heard in the past. Why did you find some of them very interesting, while others bored you almost to tears? I would bet you that the difference had more to do with the way those speakers dealt with their competition and resistance from the audience than it did with the content of their speeches.

It is often easier to identify interference than it is to cope with it. In fact, coping with the competition from distractions and dealing with resistance from the audience will take all the creativity at your disposal. You'll find that every situation is different and every audience is unique. However, as one who speaks on an average of 200 times each year, I have discovered that there are some tested and proven guidelines that can help you overcome even the worst situations and communicate effectively with even the most resistant audiences.

GET PHYSICALLY INVOLVED
WITH YOUR AUDIENCE

Hiding behind a dais or maintaining a safe distance from your audience might make you feel more secure—it might even keep the audience from seeing your shaky knees—but it won't help you connect with your audience.

All communication is dialog, and no dialog can take place between a speaker and an audience that are isolated from each other. By crashing through the physical barriers of objects and space that separate you from your audience, you can overcome stiff competition and strong resistance.

Believe me, I've encountered some strong competition over the years. Once, when I spoke to the Associated General Contractors of America, I was scheduled to speak in the afternoon and President Ronald Reagan was scheduled to speak at mid-morning. For some reason, President Reagan had to re-schedule his talk for the exact time I was to speak. At the time, the building business was depressed because of high interest rates and tight money, so most of the people at the conference opted to go hear the President. Now that's stiff competition! It would have been easy for me to assume that, since I only had about thirty people when I had expected several hundred, it was a hopeless situation. But I realized that those people who came really wanted to hear my message, and I tried twice as hard to please them. I called them up to the front of the room, seated them around a large table, and we had a group discussion. They got so involved that it was hard to break it off at the appointed time.

The difference in the words "united" and "untied" is where you place the "i" in the words. Where you place yourself in relation to your audience can determine how that audience will receive you. If you isolate yourself from them, you and that audience will remain *untied;* if you physically connect with them, you and they will become *united.*

GET YOUR AUDIENCE
PHYSICALLY INVOLVED WITH YOU

The quickest and most effective way to connect with your audience is to get them to do things with you. Even when strong barriers exist, they can be broken down by either getting the whole audience to do something, or calling an individual from the audience up front to do something before the whole crowd.

I spoke at Western Kentucky University for their Free Enterprise Fair and shared the platform with Dave Thomas, who founded Wendy's, and Bill Leonard, who was then the president of CBS News. Our audience was made up of several thousand students from area high schools who were there primarily for a good time. I had spoken six times that week to major corporations and association groups, and I knew that I would have to change my style of connecting with the audience if I stood any chance of breaking through to that crowd.

I began with a clapping game in which I always get the audience to clap when my hands cross before them, and not to clap when my hands don't cross. The idea is to fake crossing my hands, and to keep speeding up the tempo until I have them confused. I kept working at it until every person in the auditorium was clapping with the crossing of my hands. Pretty soon, they were laughing and thoroughly involved with what I had to say.

The results of exercises with your audience can sometimes be hilarious. Once, when I spoke at the River Oaks Country Club in Houston, I asked how many of the men present dominated their wives. Only one guy raised his hand. That brought a big laugh. But it was not nearly so funny as when his wife stood up and pushed his arm down.

When you involve one person from the audience, that whole audience identifies with that person—particularly if it is a person who is known and loved by everybody in the group. The old magicians obviously knew more about connecting with an audience than simply doing sleight-of-hand tricks. They would often call for a volunteer from the audience to come up and help them with a trick. They knew that the tactic would help them establish both credibility and connection with their audiences.

There are two cautions about working with an individual before an audience. First, make sure the person has a good sense of humor and, if possible, that you have cleared it with them before you call them up. Second, since the audience identifies more with the person than they do with you, be careful never to embarrass or put down the person. When you have finished with the person, compliment him or her on being a good sport and ask the audience to give them a round of applause. This gets the whole audience involved, makes the individual feel good, and identifies you with the audience.

Here are some tips for involving your audience with you:

1. Keep it simple.
2. Make it move.
3. Keep it short.

4. Make it fun for everyone.
5. Make it fit your audience and situation.

Most professional trainers develop their own exercises for getting people involved with them because they want to find tactics that fit their own personalities and styles. However, there are several good books available that contain many good exercises you can adapt.

ANIMATE YOUR PRESENTATION

Experts say that at least seventy percent of what we communicate is communicated non-verbally—which means that how you say things is usually more important than what you say.

Remember this: *everything you say, and everything you do communicates something to your audience.* Arms hanging down your sides like spaghetti tell your audience you are scared to death. Arms folded across your chest say to that audience that you are defensive. Hands nervously fidgeting with your glasses or notes communicate extreme self-consciousness.

If you want your audience to relax and get into what you are saying, then relax and get into what you are saying. If you would like them to become active in their listening and response, then be animated in your presentation. Nothing communicates like enthusiasm! And nothing conveys enthusiasm like animation. People can tell from the tone of your voice, your volume modulation, and the expressions on your face how strongly you believe what you are saying and how much you want to communicate it to them.

Practice, practice, practice, and you can become a very animated speaker—even if you tend to be inhibited. Practice saying things with expression. Practice using gestures to good advantage. Practice handling a microphone until you can do it naturally and without making it pop.

When you are before an audience, let yourself go. Let all of the winning ways of your personality come through. Your audience may not become as animated as you'd like for them to, but they will never become more animated than you do.

CUSTOM FIT YOUR STYLE
TO YOUR AUDIENCE

Obviously, you have to use a little common sense in making your presentation. It would not be appropriate for a minister to get his audience involved in a clapping game at a funeral; nor would you want to involve a group of physically handicapped people in vigorous physical exercises.

Many people can still remember the opening of Gabriel Heater's news commentaries during World War II. If our troops had fared well, he'd open up his newscast with, "Ah! There's good news tonight!" If things had gone badly for them, his opening remark would be, "Ah! There's bad news tonight!" Everything about his words and tone of voice set you up to hear what he had to say. And many Americans didn't feel they had really heard the truth about the war until they had heard it from Gabriel Heater.

Watch Dr. Robert Schuller sometime as he addresses the large audience at the Crystal Cathedral and presents it on nationwide television. He parades up and down the high platform, speaks with a booming voice, and accents everything he says with a grandiose gesture. Then, when the camera closes in tightly on him and he gives a "personal message" to people on television, he uses intimate gestures, looks right into the camera, and talks as if you are the only person he is addressing.

Skilled communicators give you the feeling that everything they say is meant for your ears alone, that you matter more than anyone in the world at that moment, and that what they have to say to you is of vital importance. It's their way of breaking through the walls of competition and resistance that greet every person who would attempt to communicate.

ACCENT WITH VISUALS

With television and all of its derivatives becoming increasingly popular, ours is a very visually-oriented society. In fact, the experts tell us that eighty-five percent of what we learn is learned through our eyes. Think a little bit about what that implies to a person who would seek to communicate verbally. Not only does it mean that there is tremendous power in visual communication; it means that the greatest sources of distraction are visible.

Therefore, if you want to crash through the barriers of competition and resistance, the most effective way to do it is with visuals. The reason most people will come to hear a speaker, rather than simply listening to that speaker on a tape, is that they want to see the person who is speaking. Controlling the attention of your audience also means controlling their eyes. That is why animation is so important.

Many effective communicators add visual stimulation to their presentations in order to get their audiences more completely involved. For example, one approach I've used is to display several common items (a key, a paper clip, a cup, a pencil, etc.) on an opaque projector. After I've given the audience a minute to observe them, I will turn off the projector and ask them to write down a list of all the things displayed. Then I lead into a discussion of how little we tend to observe the common things around us and how hard it is to remember even a few things.

Here are some pointers that can help you use visuals to good advantage:

1. Keep them simple (never more than three lines on a slide).
2. Convey only one message per visual.
3. Make sure the visual calls attention to you and your message, rather than distracting your audience.
4. Practice using the visuals until you can do it comfortably.
5. Make sure they will work before the presentation begins.
6. Keep them short.
7. Apply them to what you are saying.
8. Test the audience's response to them.

The most common problem with using visuals is that they call attention to themselves, rather than to the speaker and what is being said. I find it helpful to think of them as waiters bringing in their message, and then disappearing.

DON'T WEAR OUT YOUR WELCOME

Say what you have to say, as effectively as you can say it, and always within the allotted time; then quit!

Every person who attempts to communicate encounters interference in the form of competition or resistance, or both. The real pros are the ones who can break through the barriers and involve their audiences with them.

The examples and illustrations we have used in this chapter have been primarily from the situations of public speakers, but the principles behind them can be applied to almost any kind of communication. If you would become an effective communicator, first you must understand interference and be able to identify its source. Then you must be able to cope with it either through eliminating it, or through a strategy for making it work for you instead of against you.

GROWTH EXERCISES

1. Select a recent attempt you made to communicate (through any medium) that was less than successful and analyze how competition or resistance might have blocked it. Were there any insights gained from this chapter that might have enabled you to break through the barriers more effectively?

2. Identify interference by its source in one each of the following categories from your recent attempts to communicate:

Competition from the environment
Emotional or intellectual resistance from the audience

Analyze how you could have dealt with that interference more effectively.

3. Describe how you have done each of the following in communicating with various audiences, and analyze how you could have done them more effectively.

- Get physically involved with your audience.
- Get your audience physically involved with you.
- Animate your presentations.
- Custom fit your style to your audience.
- Accent with visuals.
- Don't wear out your audience.

CHAPTER SIX

CREATIVE LISTENING: THE EFFECTIVE COMMUNICATOR'S WINNING EDGE

Effective communication is always a two-way street—drive down that street in the wrong lane and you're headed for a collision with your audience. The person who would learn to communicate effectively must first learn how to listen effectively.

During the Great Depression of the thirties, a young man who had been out of work for a long time saw a "help wanted" ad for a telegraph operator and went immediately to apply for the position. He had no experience, but had studied Morse code at home during the time he'd been unemployed; he was sure he could do the job if given the chance.

As he walked into the reception area of the telegraph office, his heart sank within him. There sat more than twenty-five people busily filling out application blanks. Glancing over the shoulders of some of the applicants, he saw that they had had many years of experience. Disappointed, he sat down to fill out his application blank.

Suddenly, the young man jumped to his feet and rushed through the door into the office. Soon a man appeared in the doorway and made a shocking announcement.

"I'm sorry," he said, "the position has just been filled."

"But I don't understand," protested one of the applicants. "That guy came in after all of us. . . . What did he say that made you hire him?"

"He didn't say anything," came the reply. "He listened to

what we were saying!" Then the man explained that for more than an hour he had been tapping a message in Morse Code on the other side of a glass panel separating the office from the reception area, and the young man was the first to respond to its invitation.

The message? It simply said, "If you understand this, come on in. The job is yours!"

All the other applicants had been so busy writing down all the things they wanted to say about themselves that they had failed to listen to their prospective employer. Listening was the young man's winning edge.

Too many attempts to communicate can only be described as "monologues in duet." (That's when you think up what you are going to say while someone is saying what he or she thought up while you were talking.)

COMMUNICATION IS A HAZARDOUS PURSUIT

Someone has defined communication as a "meeting of meanings." The word communication comes from a Latin word meaning "to make common."

It sounds very simple, doesn't it? But consider this communications puzzler: "I know you think you understand what you thought I said, but I'm not sure that what you thought you heard is what I meant to say."

Part of the difficulty in conveying messages accurately stems from the use of words themselves. The 500 most common words in the English language have more than 14,000 meanings—an average of twenty-eight meanings per word. To further complicate things, those meanings change constantly from time to time and from person to person. Add to that the fact that there are more than 700,000 kinds of non-verbal communication, and the process of exchanging information and ideas becomes very complex.

As if that were not enough to complicate communications, many messages are poorly sent and many more are poorly received. Thus, we say things we don't mean, mean things we don't say, and understand things others don't mean to say.

All of that adds up to put a premium on listening actively

to every person with whom we would communicate. Those who learn to do it well find it's the key to solving many problems, strengthening many valuable relationships, avoiding many conflicts, and being able to work more productively and happily.

Let's look more specifically at some of the more outstanding benefits of active listening:

BENEFITS OF ACTIVE LISTENING

BENEFIT #1: WHEN WE ACTIVELY LISTEN, WE CAN LEARN.   "Every man I meet is in some way my superior, and, in that, I can learn of him," said the wise Emerson.

BENEFIT #2: WHEN WE ACTIVELY LISTEN, WE EXPRESS INTEREST IN THE PERSON TO WHOM WE LISTEN.   By actively listening we can affirm that the person has value to us: that they matter.

BENEFIT #3: WHEN WE ACTIVELY LISTEN, WE GAIN INSIGHT AS TO HOW THE PERSON PERCEIVES HIS OR HER NEEDS, DESIRES, AND MOTIVATIONS. Often our perceptions of what makes people act the way they do, and react to us the way they do, are vastly different from what those people actually feel. We tend to judge others by their words and actions, while we judge ourselves by our motivations. By listening we are able to narrow the gap between what we think and what they think.

BENEFIT #4: WHEN WE ACTIVELY LISTEN, WE GIVE PEOPLE AN OPPORTUNITY TO LET DOWN THEIR GUARDS SO THEY CAN HEAR WHAT WE HAVE TO SAY.   The person who feels that he or she has been heard is much more receptive to hearing what the listener has to say.

BENEFIT #5: WHEN WE ACTIVELY LISTEN, WE ACTIVELY INVOLVE THE OTHER PERSON IN THE COMMUNICATIONS PROCESS WE WANT TO TAKE PLACE. The person who sits with defiant expression, arms crossed over the chest, and locked up ears is not involved in our attempt at dialog. Our only hope of getting the person involved, so that together we might move to a new reality, is to get that person to open up. The best way to do that is to listen.

TIONS.   Often, we reject what people are saying, because we misunderstand what they mean. These explanations of how accidents
occurred, taken from actual insurance forms, can illustrate the problem of taking literally what people say:

"The telephone pole was approaching fast, I was attempting
to swerve out of its path when it struck my front end." (Those
poles can chase you down!)

"I had been driving my car for four years when I fell
asleep at the wheel and had an accident." (That's got to be a
record!)

"I was on my way to the doctor's with rear end trouble when
my universal joint gave way causing me to have an accident." (Really? What kind of doctor?)

"To avoid hitting the bumper of the car in front, I struck
the pedestrian." (I bet that pedestrian got sore!)

Sometimes it takes a lot of active listening to hear what people
are trying to tell us. The other side of the coin is that people
reject what we say because we don't adequately convey what we
mean. Sometimes we can be as clumsy as the fellow who was trying
to compliment his hostess.

"Your daughter is beautiful," he said (and should have quit).
"She's even prettier than you!"

Realizing how that must have sounded, he quickly attempted
a recovery.

"That's not what I meant," he stumbled. "Actually, she's not
pretty at all."

Unfortunately, many of the misconceptions that make it hard
for us to communicate effectively are not so humorous. Sometimes
they can cause loss, pain, and grief. It is only when we actively
listen that we can hear, and clear up, misconceptions.

HOW GOOD A LISTENER ARE YOU?

Right now you might be thinking, "Who needs all this talk about
listening? I'm a good listener!" Are you, really? Let me suggest
that you first take the following test yourself, then ask two of the
people with whom you communicate most frequently to rate you
on the same statements.

Listening Test

(Number a sheet of paper from 1 to 20, then rate yourself on a scale of 1 [low rating] to 5 [high rating] on each of the following statements. Ask two friends to rate you on the same scale and compare your findings.)

1. I always attempt to give every person I talk with equal time to talk.
2. I really enjoy hearing what other people have to say.
3. I never have difficulty waiting until someone finishes talking so that I can have my say.
4. I listen even when I do not particularly like the person talking.
5. The sex and age of a person makes no difference in how well I listen.
6. I assume every person has something worthwhile to say and listen intently to friends, acquaintances, and strangers alike.
7. I put away what I am doing while someone is talking.
8. I always look directly at the person who is talking and give that person my full attention, no matter what is on my mind.
9. I encourage others to talk by giving them verbal feedback and asking questions.
10. I encourage other people to talk by my non-verbal messages, such as gestures, facial expressions, and posture.
11. I ask for clarification of words and ideas I do not understand.
12. I am sensitive to the tone of the speaker's voice, expressions, and gestures that convey meaning.
13. I never interrupt a person who is talking.
14. I withhold all judgements and opinions about what a person is saying until I have heard it all.
15. I listen past the words to the feelings and meanings the person is expressing, and test to see if I am understanding correctly.
16. I make mental outlines of the main points of what a person is saying.
17. I look mainly for points on which we can agree, not mainly for points on which we disagree.
18. I respect every person's right to his or her opinions, even if I disagree with them.
19. I view every dispute or conflict as an opportunity to understand the person better.
20. I recognize that listening is a skill and I concentrate on trying to develop that skill in my daily life.

SCORING: Add up the total point value of your ratings and score them as follows: 90–100, You're all ears; 80–89, You're a pretty good listener; 70–79, You're missing a lot; and 69 and under, it might be a good idea to have your ears checked.

The fact is that all of us can improve our skills at listening. It is equally true that by improving our skills at listening, we can improve our skills as communicators.

THREE GREAT BARRIERS
TO ACTIVE LISTENING

Just as we attempt to send messages and encounter barriers, we tend to erect barriers that keep us from hearing what others have to say to us. By understanding these barriers and discovering some techniques for dealing with them, we can not only become better listeners but understand more about why people fail to listen to us.

Barrier # 1: Preconceived Notions

The most common barrier we erect is preconceived notions. We approach others with biases, prejudices, and opinions—many of them false.

I'm sure you have heard brilliant talks that were magnificently delivered but accomplished nothing. The most common failure of speakers is that they fail to get in touch with what their audiences are really feeling. They make assumptions based on what they know or think rather than attempting to find out what the audience thinks.

Barrier #2: Haste

It takes time to listen to other people, and far too often we are not willing to invest the time necessary to get in touch with other people.

Someone once said that active listening is the most loving thing one person can do for another. When we actively listen, we take the time to demonstrate that we really care about the other person.

Most of us tend to suffer from "agenda anxiety," the feeling that what we want to say to others is more important than what we think they might want to say to us. It is only when we are willing to put aside our fears, desires, and self-centeredness that we can become good listeners.

TIPS ON GOOD LISTENING

If you're really serious about becoming an effective communicator, first you must become an effective listener. Here are some tips that can help you do exactly that:

Tip #1: Be open! Switch off all negative thoughts about the person. Be receptive to what is being said. Drop those emotional barriers that filter out what is being said or cause you to hear only what you want to hear.

Tip #2: Start listening with the first sentence! Self-centered people can't actively listen. They tend to be preoccupied with their own daydreams. Put aside what you are doing and concentrate on what the person is saying.

Tip #3: Concentrate on what is being said! Actively try to hear every word as if it were the most important thing you could hear at that moment. Avoid the temptation to think faster than the person is talking.

Tip #4: Look for the meaning of what is being said. Don't try to read your own meanings into what the person is saying. Rather, help the person convey his or her own meanings by showing genuine interest.

Tip #5: Avoid the temptation to interrupt! Dr. David Schwartz, in his book *The Magic Of Thinking Big*, says, "Big people monopolize the listening. Small people monopolize the talking."

Tip #6: Ask questions that stimulate the person to talk and clarify your understanding of what is being said. Use trail questions, like "Do I understand correctly that . . . ," to test your understanding.

Tip #7: File away important points being made. If appropriate, take notes.

Tip #8: Screen out interruptions and ignore distractions.

Tip #9: Use facial expressions and body language to express interest and comprehension.

Tip #10: Don't over-react to highly charged or emotional words; look for the meanings behind those words. Avoid jumping to conclusions. Hear the person out.

IGNITERS OR KILLERS

Approachability is one of the greatest qualities a communicator can possess. It opens the door for new ideas, deeper relationships, and better understanding. One of the keys to opening ourselves to others is using "igniter" phrases, that is, responses that make people want to talk to us. When we use "killer phrases," we close off the channels of communication.

Below are two lists: one shows igniter phrases that make us approachable, and the other shows killer phrases that tend to close us off from other people:

IGNITER PHRASES	KILLER PHRASES
I like that!	The problem with that idea is . . .
Keep talking, you're on track.	No way it will work here.
Go ahead . . . try it.	Impossible under our current system.
Keep going!	We just can't get support for it!
We can do a lot with that idea.	It's not a bad idea, but . . .
That's great, how can we do it?	We've never done it that way before.
That's neat, what else do we need?	You haven't considered . . .
How can we get support for it?	We have too many projects now!
What else do we need to consider?	A swell idea, but . . .
I think it will fly!	It won't work!
Gee, why not!	We haven't the time!
Wow! Let's try it!	It's not in the budget!
Where would we be without you?	We've tried that before!
Hey, that's a great idea!	Not ready for it yet!
How can we build on that idea?	All right in theory, but can you put it into practice!

IGNITER PHRASES	KILLER PHRASES
Let's get right on it.	It needs more study.
I know it will work!	Somebody would have suggested it before if it were any good!
Why not!	Let's discuss it at some other time.
That's the way to go!	You don't understand our problem!
How can we help you?	Why start anything now?
This is going to be fun!	You know, I think you really ARE dumb!
I love challenges like this!	Has anyone else ever tried it?
That's like you!!!	I just know it won't work!
I agree!	Let's be practical!
Let's go!	Let's form a committee.
That would be interesting to try!	It's been the same for ten years, why change now?
That's good!	Why can't you come up with something good?
That's a great idea!	What's the use of trying it?
I'm glad you brought that up.	
That's an interesting idea.	
It's sure nice to have you with us!	
Look out world, here we come!	

TYING IT ALL TOGETHER

The person who would get others to pay attention and really listen to what he or she has to say must first be willing to listen to what others have to say. Active listening is a skill that can be learned and cultivated. It is something we do out of caring and concern for other people, but it carries with it some strong benefits for us.

All of us can improve our listening skills; and by improving the frequency and depth at which we listen we can improve our effectiveness as communicators. In fact, our ability to approach others with our messages and requests is directly related to how approachable we are.

GROWTH EXERCISES

1. Select a person with whom you've had some difficulty in communicating and set up a plan for breaking through the barriers that separate you. The plan should include goals for listening, strategies for implementing those goals, and indications by which you will know when communication improves.

2. Select a person whom you know very well and seek to learn at least three significant things about that person by applying the techniques we discussed in the section on "Tips on Good Listening."

3. The next time you are approached by a stranger, practice actively listening to that stranger and see how much you can learn about the person. After you have listened to the person, make a list of things you learned about him or her, and list at least one valuable insight about life you gained by listening to the person.

CHAPTER SEVEN

HOW TO TARGET YOUR AUDIENCE

A couple strolls hand in hand along a quiet moonlit beach. There's no one else in sight, and the only sound they hear is the lapping of the gentle waves upon the sand beneath their bare feet. As if by a prearranged signal, they stop, slowly turn to face each other, and he speaks.

"I love you," he says softly.

"I love you, too," she replies.

"Will you marry me?" he asks.

"Oh, yes!" she responds with deep emotion.

For a long time they gaze into each other's eyes. Slowly they come together in a kiss, then hand in hand they stroll on down the beach.

That, my friend, is effective communication! It was the right person, saying the right thing, to the right audience, at the right time, in the right way, to be heard and understood, and it produced the desired response.

They spoke only four short sentences, containing thirteen words; but they changed the lives of two people forever.

Contrast that story with this one:

A young man once fell madly in love with a young lady and decided he wanted to make her his wife. So strong was his affection for her that he pledged, although he scarcely knew her, he would marry her within one year.

Since he was very bashful, he started sending her a letter

every day. For one full year there was never a day that went by but the mailman delivered a letter to her from him, telling her of his undying love for her.

Sure enough, on the last day of that year, she consented to give her hand in marriage—*to the mailman!*

The young man produced action, but it was not the action he desired.

Far too many would-be communicators use a "scattergun" approach in conveying their messages. You'll see them cornering anyone who will listen to them, throwing words at them in hopes some of them will strike a responsive chord, and hoping the people they talk to will do something. They become frustrated, disappointed, and feel misunderstood.

Effective communications are a result of skillful targeting— targeting of your audience, targeting of your subject, targeting of your presentation, and targeting of the response you desire. We will look at each of these much more carefully in this section of the book. In this particular chapter, let's target targeting your audience.

TARGET FOR EFFECTIVENESS

Join me in a little word-association game that could change your whole approach to communicating.

When I say the word "target," what's the first word that comes to mind?

"Bullseye!" You've got it!

The most universally recognized image of a target is the traditional "bullseye" because everything about it literally pulls your eye to one focal point—the dot in the center of its decreasing circles. Whether you are throwing darts, shooting an arrow, or using a firearm the principle works the same: you aim for the dot in the center and attempt to come as close to it as you can.

If you are competing with other people in targeting, you attempt to come closer to the bullseye more often than your competitors. Those who hit the center of the target most often are the winners.

The same principles work in communicating effectively with audiences.

Those who want to communicate effectively zero-in on the audience they want to reach with their messages, and those who reach those targets most often become the real pros at it.

As we saw in chapter five, communicators often compete with distractions from the environment in which they try to reach their audience. One key to reaching your targeted audience more often than the competition caused by "interference" is targeting your audiences very carefully.

WHY IS TARGETING NECESSARY?

Recently, a man drove up to the Washington Monument in a large van which he claimed was loaded with dynamite. Threatening to blow up the landmark, he held off guards and police for almost a full day and attracted news media from around the world. When asked why he was doing it, the man replied that it was to initiate "a national dialog on nuclear disarmament."

As the Federal Bureau of Investigation and the various news-gathering agencies looked into the background of the man they discovered that he had spent his productive energies for many years attempting to get a "national dialog" going with anyone who would listen. Unfortunately, he had not been successful, so he had decided to make one last desperate attempt.

Finally, as he started to drive the truck away from the monument, police sharpshooters opened fire and killed him.

"He had told a reporter that all he wanted to do was call attention to the dangers of nuclear warfare," said one news commentator who was analyzing the incident later that evening. "Sadly," she continued, "all he did was to call attention to himself."

It's a pattern that is being repeated increasingly in our nation and around the world—people trying to attract an audience to hear their message but only succeeding in attracting attention to themselves.

You've seen them, I'm sure: people who dress in bizarre clothing to "make a statement," people who publicly stage death-defying stunts to attract the cameras, and people engaging in all sorts of anti-social acts because they have not been able to make significant contact with those who matter in their lives.

Of course, it's not a new phenomenon. The *New Yorker* magazine has been running cartoons for several decades that show the ever-present guy with his sign proclaiming that "The End Is Near." To a lesser degree, all of us are faced with the challenge of connecting with audiences that matter to us. To some extent, we all know the frustration of feeling that our messages are not being heard.

None of us likes to be ignored. Perhaps that's why the people who make deodorants, toothpaste, and beauty aids bombard us with their messages; and maybe that's why they are so successful in selling us their products. To be ignored is to be rejected, and none of us likes that.

Now, don't get me wrong! With some of the people I meet, I'm all in favor of soaps, deodorants, mouthwashes, and anything that will make them look and smell better. It's just that there is a far more common reason our messages are not heard by those we would like to hear them: we somehow fail to connect with the right audiences for our messages.

As a communications consultant to some of America's top business and professional leaders, I find that one of the most common reasons their attempts to communicate fail is that they are addressing the wrong people with their messages. The entrepreneurs who sold "pet rocks" by the thousands a few years ago proved that if you connect with the right audience you can convey almost any message you desire and get the response you want.

Let's face it, we simply cannot communicate with everyone in the world—even if we feel we have the most powerful message the world has ever heard. At best, we can connect with a very limited number of audiences. Those who become the real pros at communicating learn to zero-in on those audiences they can realistically expect to reach. They learn to target very specifically and go for the dot in the center of the bullseye.

BENEFITS OF TARGETING YOUR AUDIENCE

P. T. Barnum once said that half the money he spent on promoting his circuses was wasted, but since he could never be sure which half, he continued to spend it all. That dilemma might have something to do with why the circus has all but disappeared from the complex American scene.

In today's economy, advertising costs too much for people to waste it on audiences they hope to reach. Modern advertising agencies go to great lengths to determine the cost/effectiveness ratio of the money their clients spend trying to get their messages across to their potential customers.

Targeting audiences is becoming an exact science with people who want to become effective communicators. When you look at some of the benefits, it is easy to understand why the real pros zero-in and try to reach the audiences they want to reach.

BENEFIT #1: BY TARGETING, YOU CAN CONCENTRATE ALL YOUR ENERGIES AND RESOURCES INTO ONE FOCAL POINT.   When I was a little boy, my brother gave me a small magnifying glass. I soon discovered that it had some strange powers. When I held it a certain distance from an object it made that object look bigger, so I could get a better look at it. By magnifying what I was looking at, it enabled me to see it more clearly.

But I soon discovered that little glass had another wonderful power. When I held it up to the sun's rays, and focused it exactly right, it would concentrate all the sun's rays coming through it into one tiny little dot that was very bright. If I held it in the same spot for a few seconds, it would burn a hole in the object it was focused upon.

It was an exhilarating discovery! Suddenly, I could see things more clearly than I had ever seen them, and I could harness the sun's power to work for me.

As a professional communicator, those discoveries have proved very valuable to me. *They have taught me that targeted power is concentrated power, and concentrated power is amplified power.*

When you concentrate all your energies and resources onto targeted audiences, you are able to understand them better, give more of yourself to them, and bring to bear the full power of all that you have and all that you are to reach those audiences. The result is that you become much more powerful as a communicator.

BENEFIT #2: TARGETING GIVES PURPOSE AND DIRECTION TO YOUR COMMUNICATIONS EFFORTS.   This is an age of specialization—and for good reason. We are in the midst of a knowledge explosion with so much information being added each year that only those who specialize can keep up with it all. Thus, specialized audiences are increasingly looking for those communicators who can speak to them with authority about their fields of endeavor.

By zeroing-in on a limited number of audiences you can invest all your time and energies in becoming acquainted with the unique needs, desires, and motivations of those audiences. As you become increasingly aware of those audiences it is easier to develop your skills and techniques for reaching them.

Look, for example, at the field of direct mail advertising. Those people who have really been successful there are the ones who have studied carefully the types of mailing lists that draw the best response for them. By understanding the people on those lists, and the best approaches for reaching them, they have been able to sharpen their skills at communicating with fewer people— at lower costs—and selling to more of them.

BENEFIT #3: BY TARGETING YOUR AUDIENCES, YOU BECOME KNOWN BY THOSE YOU WOULD REACH.   Three decades ago, the magazine industry was dominated by half-a-dozen giant mass circulation magazines. Look at the typical newsrack now and you will find that most of the giants have been replaced by highly specialized magazines which serve limited audiences. Publishers of magazines know that to be successful today they must not only direct their editorial efforts and promotion toward a specific type of audience, they must find a unique niche within that limited audience. The articles and pictures they run must appeal to the people who have come to look to them for information and entertainment of a very specialized nature.

When you, as a writer, speaker, consultant, or any other type of communicator, become widely known and respected by your chosen audiences, you will have little difficulty getting people to pay attention to you.

BENEFIT #4: BY TARGETING SPECIFIC AUDIENCES, YOU CAN SAVE YOUR MOST VALUABLE ASSET—TIME.   When you choose the specific audiences you wish to reach and concentrate entirely on those audiences, you control your time rather than allowing your time to control you.

Perhaps you're one of those people who always seems to be in a hurry and never has enough time to get things done. If so, I've got good news and I've got bad news for you.

First, the bad news—there's not going to be any more time than you have right now. There will always be only twenty-four hours in each day, and only seven days in each week.

Now for the good news—you don't really need any more time than you have. The secret to success lies in utilizing the time you have to maximum advantage.

Targeting your audiences can help you tremendously in that effort. For example, some salespeople work long hours at a feverish pace, and with very little success. They give their sales pitch to any person, anywhere, who will listen. But the truly successful salespeople concentrate on those few prospects who have a logical reason for buying, the resources and authority to buy, and a need for their product or service. They spend their time with those people who can, and are most likely to, give them the response they desire.

BENEFIT #5: BY TARGETING YOUR AUDIENCES, YOU ARE ABLE TO PRACTICE WHAT YOU DO ENOUGH TO BECOME REALLY GOOD AT IT. Someone once said, "When you do what it is you do well enough that the people who see you do it will want to see you do it again, and will bring others to see you do it, your success is guaranteed."

Practice improves your batting average. As a professional speaker, I have learned what types of stories draw a good response from certain audiences, what kinds of exercises draw them into my presentation, and how to cope with the most common interference I encounter. Thus, I am able to eliminate those stories and exercises that I know won't work and practice on those that will work until I can do them automatically. This frees me to concentrate entirely on my audience and how they are responding to what I'm doing.

Just as you become familiar with the house or apartment you live in day after day, so you become acquainted with the audiences you spend your time with day after day—but only if you concentrate on a limited number of audiences.

BENEFIT #6: BY TARGETING YOUR AUDIENCES, YOU CAN MULTIPLY YOUR EFFECTIVENESS THROUGH SPIN-OFFS. The person who communicates only once, and in only one way, with an audience misses tremendous opportunities for personal and professional growth. That person also misses tremendous opportunities to capitalize on spin-off communications.

I count on invitations for return engagements, and additional projects for clients, as the backbone of my professional speaking career. If I had to spend a high percentage of my time cultivating new audiences and developing new approaches for reaching audiences I know nothing about, I would be wasting my most creative energies.

Any time you can take a piece of communication you have developed for a limited audience and use it with very little alteration as another approach to that audience, or other very similar audiences, you can multiply your effectiveness several times over.

BENEFIT #7: BY TARGETING YOUR AUDIENCES, YOU CAN INVEST YOUR LIFE WHERE YOU HAVE THE HIGHEST INTEREST LEVEL. It's a proven fact that most people do best at the things they enjoy most doing. When you choose to speak to audiences you enjoy communicating with about subjects in which you are vitally interested, you can have the best of both worlds. You can be most effective, and you can enjoy what you do.

Play has often been defined as doing something you enjoy doing. According to this definition, you can play your way through life—and still be very successful—if you choose carefully the audiences you will target.

Too many people lead what Thoreau called "lives of quiet desperation" by getting locked into communicating with audiences they feel are thrust upon them by circumstances, or because they lack the courage to go after the audience they really wish to target. Life is too short for us to allow our audiences to target us and dictate how we will spend our time.

Whether your medium of communication is music, art, writing, or speaking, you owe it to yourself and the world to invest your talents with the audiences that will respond to your highest level of interest.

HOW TO TARGET YOUR AUDIENCE

Okay, so targeting is necessary if you want to become an effective communicator, and there are many benefits to be derived from zeroing-in on specific audiences. But how do you do it? How do you select the audiences with which you will invest your most creative communications efforts?

There are five questions to ask yourself that can help you get a clear focus on which audiences should get the most of your attention.

WHAT DO I WANT TO DO?

Whether you are deciding your goals for your entire life, feeling frustrated because something you bought does not work and you want to tell somebody about it, or composing a song, the first step is always deciding exactly what you want to accomplish through your communication.

The masses of people are poor communicators because they ramble all over the place. They're like swamps that run shallow and fill every bog their waters can reach. When they've finished talking to you, or writing you a letter, all they've accomplished is to leave you confused, and maybe upset.

But the real pros at communication learn how to get things sorted out in their own minds before they reach out to tell somebody about it. They're like rivers that run in deep channels. They have depth, clarity, purpose, and direction. And you can follow them, because they know where they're going.

As a businessman, I receive letters from people who want "a job." They're usually addressed "Dear Sirs," and since no one by that name works for me, they usually end up on my desk. "I'm looking for a job. Do you have any openings?" they often start out. Unfortunately, there are a lot of people looking for jobs. "I can do many different things," they continue. I don't mean to be cold, but so can most of the people who walk in off the streets.

Since I admire anybody who makes a legitimate attempt to get gainful employment rather than letting the world support them, I usually write them a "Sorry, but no" letter before I throw their inquiries into the round file.

There's not much of a market for people who can do "a little bit of everything," but there's a crying need for people who can do a few things very well.

As we shall see later, communications that get their desired response from the selected audiences are the ones which tell those audiences specifically what you want them to do. However, before you can decide what you want your audiences to do, or even who your audiences will be, you must decide what it is you want to accomplish.

It might sound to you as if I'm belaboring a point, but, believe me, one of the most common reasons communications attempts fail is that the people who initiate them don't know what they want to accomplish. They might have a general idea—like the man who threatened to blow up the Washington Monument because he wanted to start a dialog on nuclear war—but their goals are so vague that no one can understand them. Therefore, they have no logical audience.

Get specific! What do you want to accomplish? One technique I have found helpful for making this decision is to write, in one concise sentence, precisely what I want to do. Once this has been done, I am ready to move on to the next big question.

WHO CAN BEST HELP ME GET IT DONE?

The best audience for any communication is the audience that can provide you the most help in doing what you want to do. For example, if you've bought a product which you feel has not performed satisfactorily, and you have decided what you want to do about it, you are ready to communicate with the person most likely to help you get it done. If you want the product repaired, you will probably follow the warranty instructions and send it to the indicated address. If you feel the product was misrepresented to you, and want your money back, you might communicate with the Better Business Bureau. If it has malfunctioned and injured you, and you want to see if you have grounds for a suit, you will talk to a lawyer. If you're just furious and want the store manager shot, maybe you should talk to the Mafia.

Again, deciding who can best help you do what you want to get done might sound like such an obvious step that it deserves little attention. Yet, many of the communications attempts that fail do so because they are addressed to people who cannot, or logically will not, help the communicator get done what he or she wants done.

Let me illustrate. Some of the hardest working salespeople I have met in my seminars were dismal failures. Why? As I talked with them, it became clear to me that they were running around all over the place, telling their stories to anyone who would listen. As a result, they wasted most of their time talking to people who could not buy what they had to sell. When they learned how to determine who could best make the decisions they wanted them to make—in other words, to target their audience—they were able to sell more in less time, and with less effort.

The proper question is not "Who will give me a sympathetic hearing?" but "Who is the best person, or group of persons, to give me the results I desire?"

And, that brings us to the next big question to ask yourself.

WHY WOULD THEY WANT
TO HELP ME DO IT?

One of the greatest secrets in successful targeting of audiences is in being able to answer clearly the big question that is sure to arise: "What's in it for me?"

Remember this: *people do things for their reasons, not yours or mine!*

The real pros at communicating know that their best chances of getting things done lie with those people who have the strongest reasons for doing what they will be asking them to do.

Persuading people to do things is a little like the ancient Oriental self-defense system called "judo." Those who study the martial arts are taught never to resist superior strength or struggle with resistance, but to seek to use the enemy's strength to their own advantage. Hopefully, the people you are attempting to persuade to do what you want done are not enemies—but the underlying principle applies. Selecting the audiences you wish to reach is much more productive when you are aware of the reasons people have for acting as you wish them to act.

This is another one of those questions that ineffective communicators often overlook but that the pros take very seriously. They know that it is more productive to concentrate most of their energies on the few people who have the strongest reasons for doing what they want done than to waste their resources on the many who might be interested.

A direct mail corporate client of mine, for example, was not as successful as they thought they should be. They were sending out mass mailers and getting minimal returns. After looking over their very specialized product line, I suggested they rent a mailing list of people who had bought similar products from other companies. "But those lists cost much more than the lists we are renting," protested the management. Reluctantly, they agreed to try my idea on a limited mailing. They were delighted to discover that their percentage of people responding was much greater than it had ever been. Their sales improved dramatically when they discovered the secret of targeting an audience that had demonstrated a desire for what they had to sell.

In my estimation, the greatest communicator who ever lived was Jesus Christ. His advice: "Don't cast your pearls before swine!" In other words, don't waste all your time telling your story to people who feel they have no need to hear it. Invest your time in telling your story to those who are most likely to give you the response you desire.

That leads us to the next question to ask yourself in targeting your audiences.

WHY WOULD THEY LISTEN TO ME?

There are so many voices crying for the attention of almost any audience you would address that it is imperative to know why they would choose to listen to your voice above all the others.

Don't be modest, and don't be egocentric—be honest with yourself! What qualifications do you have to ask them to do what you want done, and what do they have strong reasons for doing?

Maybe your greatest qualification is your position of authority, or perhaps it's the influence you hold over the audience, or your specialized knowledge about a subject of vital interest to them. It could be that you have a product or a service that is unique in what it offers them. Maybe it's simply that you are such a powerful persuader that you think you can break through all the barriers that might keep them from listening to you.

Young people who are just starting out in careers often have difficulty in finding jobs because they lack experience. They talk to prospective employers in large numbers, only to become discouraged when they are repeatedly turned down because they have no experience. Their efforts might be more productive if they would concentrate on finding an employer who would give them an opportunity, even in a field that was not exactly what they ultimately wanted to do, to gain some experience.

Whatever your story, if you are telling it repeatedly with little success, look at the possibility that you are attempting to reach audiences that simply will not listen to you. It might be more productive for you to back up and look for different audiences that might be more interested in your unique qualifications.

HOW ACCESSIBLE IS THIS AUDIENCE?

How many of your resources will be required to reach the audience you would like to reach? In other words, what's it going to cost you in time, money, and other resources to establish the kind of contact you need to have to get the effect you desire?

Are there other people who already have contact with the audience you want to reach? If so, do they have reason to help you contact their audience? For example, book or magazine publishers may be selling printed materials regularly to an audience you wish to reach. They might find it worthwhile to publish something you have written to appeal to their audience. Talk show hosts on television and radio are often looking for guests who have something interesting to say to their audiences.

In addition, there are often associations that serve some of the very people you wish to reach. If you can match your goals with theirs you would gain access to people who might otherwise be inaccessible to you.

There are many factors to be considered in answering this question, and all of them will have a direct bearing on how successful you will be in targeting audiences for maximum advantage. Generally, it is most productive to target the audiences that offer the greatest return for the amount of your resources you invest in reaching them.

Once you have answered the five questions above, and narrowed down your choices to a limited number of audiences you wish to target, it is helpful to evaluate them on the basis of the following criteria:

1. Does The Targeted Audience Have The *Authority* To Do What You Want Done? A sharply worded memo sent by a manager to an employee who has no authority to act on what is discussed is likely to stir up more negative feelings than action. Always make sure that the audience you target has the authority to give you the response you desire. Otherwise, you are wasting your resources and creating frustration for the audience.

2. Does The Targeted Audience Have The *Power* To Do What You Want Done? An industrial salesperson might be told that the "widget buyer" buys all the "widgets" for a certain company, but find out later that someone on a management level has to approve all purchases before they are made.

Sometimes there is a big difference between authority and power. An audience might have the authority to buy what you are selling but be limited in power (by money or other factors) to do what you want them to do. Your boss might have the authority to give you a raise, but there might be another person who must hear your appeal. Always make sure you are telling your story to the person, or persons, who have the power to give you what you want.

3. Does This Audience Know That It Needs To Hear What You Have To Say? A minister might assume that everyone needs to hear the message he or she has to proclaim but be disappointed with the response from that audience. If you feel an audience needs to hear what you have to say, but find that that audience is not aware of that need, you will find it more productive to focus on an audience that knows its need. It is possible to educate an audience to its need for your message—and it might be necessary—but it will take resources, resources that you might utilize more productively elsewhere.

4. Does The Targeted Audience Have A Desire To Hear What You Have To Say? A group of high school students might need to hear a motivational message on the value of higher education, but their interest in hearing it might be very low. Can you create a desire within them to hear it? If so, will that utilize resources you might more advantageously use elsewhere?

5. Is This The Best Audience To Hear What You Have To Say? For me, the best audience to hear what I have to say is the audience that has the best potential for giving the response I desire for the least amount of time and resources invested.

6. Am I The Best Person To Say This To This Audience? It might be far more productive for you to get someone else to say what you want said. I have turned down many speaking engagements because I knew there were others who could deliver a particular message to a given audience much more productively than I could. Remember, as a communicator, your goal is not to stroke your own ego but to get the response you desire. If someone else can do that better for you, look for a way to get them to do it.

7. What Potential Does This Audience Hold In Relation To My Life Goals? If you know who you are and where you are going, an occasional detour to reach out to an audience might help to fulfill some of your goals. However, it is very easy to follow one detour after another, only to find out later that you are investing your best resources in audiences that do not lead you toward the goals you have set for yourself.

TYING IT ALL TOGETHER

Targeted power is concentrated power, and concentrated power is amplified power. Your effectiveness as a communicator will be directly affected by the care with which you target your audiences. Choose them well and they will lead you toward the goals you have set for yourself; let them choose you through circumstances and your life will be shaped by others.

GROWTH EXERCISES

1. Select a recent communications attempt that you feel did not reach its goal. Use the principles of this chapter to determine if that attempt was made with the best audience you could have selected. How might you have been more successful by reaching out to another audience with your message?

2. Select a pet project you want to accomplish through communications and process it through the questions asked in the headings of this chapter. This one might take some time, but it can greatly enhance your chances of success, and it can provide a valuable learning experience.

CHAPTER EIGHT

HOW TO TARGET YOUR MESSAGE

Some of the most effective communicators in America are the producers of the "main titles" for television shows—those are the fifteen- to twenty-second grabbers they use at the beginning of shows to lock you into watching.

A network will pay $150,000 or more for a good "main title." Why? Because they know that the millions of dollars they have spent in producing a show will go down the drain unless they can grab enough TV-viewers before they flip to another network. They know that each second they can hold you, their chances of enticing you to watch thirty minutes or an hour go up in quantum leaps. And, since the size of the viewing audience determines how many commercials they can sell and for how much, a lot is riding on how good they are at drawing you into the shows.

The secret of their success in grabbing you is in *targeting their messages*.

These communicators know precisely what they want you to do, and they select the messages they know are most likely to get you to do it. Then they organize those messages in the most appealing way.

WHAT CAN TARGETING DO FOR YOU?

Targeting your message includes selecting your subject, choosing your material, and organizing your presentation.

Let's look more closely at what is expected of "main titles" because they represent so accurately the role of targeting messages in almost any communication situation.

The networks expect them to:

1. Gain attention immediately and hold it.
2. Introduce the subject to be covered in the show.
3. Set the tone, pace, and mood for the show.
4. Introduce the characters and convince your audience that they are good people to spend time with—people you can identify with.
5. Compel you to do what they want you to do.
6. Dispel any fears you have about watching the show.

In a very real way, those are the things you must accomplish to get the response you desire from almost any form of communication. An evening or two spent flipping channels to see how various "main titles" target the networks' messages could prove to be a very good investment. But be careful, they really work!

There are five basic steps required for you to target your message for maximum effect—regardless of whether you are proposing marriage, making a public speech, presenting a case in court, writing a memo to an employee, or undertaking almost any other communications task.

STEP # 1: TARGET YOUR SUBJECT

The most important consideration in choosing your subject is: What do you wish your audience to do in response to your communication? For example, if you're making a speech, do you want the audience to laugh, to cry, to feel better about themselves, to feel like trying harder, to understand something new, or to agree to something? Of course, you might want them to do several of all of those things, but unless one of them dominates it will be a pretty confused audience when you finish.

"I felt like I wanted to rush out and do something," said a person who had just heard a fiery speech, "but I didn't have the vaguest idea what!" Have mercy on your audience: know what you want them to do and tell them. Don't leave them guessing what they, according to you, should be doing.

Speak to Vital Subjects

Needs and their satisfaction are the basic ingredient of all communication between humans. If we had no unsatisfied needs we would never send messages to, nor receive messages from, other humans. Even a casual conversation with a stranger occurs as a result of some need. It may be nothing more than a need for the comfort of making contact with another person—but the need is there. It may be unwanted, resisted, and even cut short, but the fact that it exists between two human beings indicates some need on the part of both of them.

If needs are the reason people communicate with each other, your strongest topic for communication is the need felt most keenly by your audience, and ways of satisfying that need. Address a person's need in a way that indicates hope of meeting that need, and you immediately get that person's attention. Convince the person that the action you propose will satisfy that need, without ignoring other needs, and you've got the action you desire.

Speak to Subjects You Know
Something About

None of us likes to hear a person rattle on and on about a subject which he or she knows little or nothing about. If you want to communicate effectively, stick to what you know best. Your audience-response rating goes up in direct proportion to your knowledge of a subject.

I am often invited to speak to audiences on subjects about which I know little or nothing. Unless the proposed subject is one that I can easily find out enough to talk intelligently about, I usually suggest another topic, recommend a fellow speaker, or decline the invitation. I respect both my audience and my career too much to run all over the country showing my ignorance.

Another good reason for sticking to subjects you know something about is that they usually reflect your interests. You'll always be more impressive and effective in communicating about subjects in which you have a vital interest.

Speak to Subjects
that Are Manageable

The novice communicator often seeks to cover the entire history of the world in a five-minute speech, but the seasoned pro knows there is a limit to what an audience can grasp, and what a speaker can effectively present.

Have you noticed that most local newspapers refuse to run a picture of more than three or four persons? They prefer only one person. The reason is simple: the eye can only focus on limited images. Bunch twenty-five people into a single picture, and each person becomes so small that you cannot recognize anyone. Subjects for communication are like that. Try to cover too broad a subject, and the various parts of that subject become so confused that no one can understand what you are talking about. For example, if you are writing a letter of request, stick to that request. Be brief, be specific about what you are asking, and be direct in your approach to it. When you present too many requests, each of which requires some consideration, you stand a good chance of getting nothing done.

Few of us can fire "the shot heard round the world," or change the pattern of history with one short memo, or correct all the abuses we see by writing a book. It's better to chip away, a little bit at a time, with many small and precisely targeted communications.

STEP #2: COLLECT
ALL THE MATERIALS YOU NEED

The more you know about a subject, the more forcefully you can present your case. Obviously, the more complex your communications attempt, the more research you need to do.

First, get your facts straight. Nothing weakens an attempt to convey a message as much as faulty information. This is especially important if you are criticizing someone. Make sure you know what you are talking about. Don't assume, check!

Second, gather all the data you need to make a strong case. Collect quotes, specific examples, research data, and anything else that will support or help you clarify your position. Gather more than you plan to use so you can select the strongest items of information.

Third, prepare yourself by studying the materials you have gathered. You'll be surprised how much your confidence increases as you learn more about what you are attempting to communicate.

STEP #3: SELECT
THE MATERIALS YOU WILL USE

Choose the points most likely to get the response you desire. Advertising copywriters often use the term "unique selling proposition" to describe a client's most compelling point. In other words, they look for what it is that is most likely to get people to act as you wish them to act.

In most forms of communication, you can count on making only one good point. I have found that it is helpful to boil down the most important point I want to get across into a concise sentence that expresses it precisely. (That's true whether I'm writing a letter or memo, preparing a speech, writing a book, or structuring a proposal for a prospective client.) Once I have a clear focus on what I want to say, I'm better able to convey that to my audience.

Once you have selected your most compelling point, look for the materials and arguments that present it in the clearest light and support it most emphatically. Choose the images and explanations that best serve to explain any part of the point that needs clarification for your audience. Don't assume they understand everything you understand. Define your terms, explain your conclusions, and guide them to understand what you have discovered.

Select information, materials, and arguments that add the most credibility to your main point. If you know your audience, you can select the supportive materials you feel they will find most convincing. Keep paring it all down until only the essential points, ideas, arguments, and supportive data remain.

STEP #4: LET IT RIPEN
IN YOUR MIND

Most messages, like fine wines, improve with age. For example, it's reliably reported that Abraham Lincoln allowed his House Divided against Itself speech to ripen in his mind for thirty days before delivering it.

Spouting out replies to inquiries or requests for action might serve to clear your desk of important projects—it might even get the "monkey on somebody else's back"—but in the long run it might well create more work for you.

"Why is there never enough time to do it right, but always enough time to do it over?" someone asked. It's a good question. Half-baked ideas and expressions make muddled communications that often produce the opposite response from what you desire to happen.

Often, when I have an important letter to write, I will hurriedly dictate an answer. Then I will let it ripen for several days, during which time I will question everything I have said. If it's really important, I will test my statements on some people whose judgements I value. Once I feel that I have really digested what I want to say, I will then dictate a final draft. This process has helped me to avoid the consequences of poor communication in many situations.

STEP #5: ORGANIZE YOUR MESSAGE

Every significant piece of communication you seek to convey can be more effective if you organize it to accomplish precisely what you desire. When you first try this, you'll find it a laborious task. Once you've developed the habit of organizing, however, it will become second nature to you.

Here are some tips that can make organizing messages both simple and effective.

Organize Around Your Most Compelling Point

What makes the punchline of a joke funny is that it has been carefully set up by the telling of a story. In other words, the punchline is the whole reason for telling the story. Few punchlines are funny when said alone.

Likewise, your most compelling point has more impact when everything you say sets it up. That doesn't mean that your most compelling point should always be the last line of a speech, or a letter, or a memo—as the punchline is in a joke. What it does mean is that the whole communication should be organized so that the most compelling point is presented in the most powerful way.

Think of the message as a display, like a department store window. Every accent in a good window display is there for one purpose: to call attention to the merchandise to be sold. The whole arrangement is structured to call attention to one focal point—the merchandise to be sold. In a good sentence, or a good song, or a good commercial, every component exists and is arranged to call attention to its most compelling point.

At first, this approach might sound very restrictive to you; but as you experiment with it you will find it holds a wide range of possibilities. For example, you can set up the most compelling line as the opening statement and use the remainder of the communication to explain and support it. Or you can repeat the most compelling line again and again throughout the communication, using supportive material to set it up each time you use it. Or you can use the novelist's approach and build suspense until you are ready to spring the most compelling point. Whatever your technique, your goal is to display that central point to maximum advantage.

Use Three Major Components

A strong communication always has at least three major components: an introduction, a main body, and a conclusion. When you understand the purpose of each, you can use them together as a skilled artist uses paint brushes to create a finished picture.

The primary purpose of the *introduction* is to get people to pay attention to what you are about to tell them. Notice how local television stations do it with teasers for their newscasts. A typical "newsbrief" might be as follows: "Fire sweeps through a downtown hotel killing seven people . . . details at eleven." That's a real grabber! It's a good grabber because it does more than simply get your attention. It creates excitement and interest in what the station is about to tell you. It draws you into the newscast by alerting you that what follows later is of vital importance to you. Therefore, it is a good introduction.

Many communicators fail to use introductions to good advantage because they depend on them only to attract attention. I've heard speakers say something like, "Sex! Now that I have your attention, I want to talk to you about. . . ." In certain groups, it might get attention, but it does little to draw people into the speaker's remarks. Telling a good joke at the beginning of a speech often fails as an introduction because the joke has nothing to do with what is about to be said. It might get the attention of the audience, but it does little to display the most compelling point. A good introduction must always alert an audience to the fact that what is about to be said is something they should hear.

The *main body* of communication presents the most compelling point in the clearest and most stimulating light. To do that, a good main body does four things:

1. It makes the subject matter interesting—it entertains.
2. It informs or instructs—it clarifies what you have to say.
3. It persuades—it convinces the audience that what you say is true.
4. It inspires—it motivates people to act as you wish them to act.

These four functions should not be separated from each other but should be carefully interwoven throughout the entire main body. If you're making a speech, for example, it is seldom productive to start out with strong humor, then shift to a professorial approach. Audiences are fickle. As soon as the fun is over, they'll tune you out. If you use humor (and it is a strong form of entertainment), it should be sprinkled throughout the entire presentation.

The most convenient way to organize the main body of the communication is to use three main points. Again, you will want to use the structure that best presents the most compelling point. You might start out with the most compelling point, and then use point two to explain it and point three to convince the audience to act in relation to it. Or, you can use points one and two to set it up, and present the unique selling proposition as point three. Use your imagination, and try several possible arrangements before you commit to a final outline; but always present the most compelling point in its most convincing setting.

A *conclusion* is exactly what its name implies—it is an ending for the communication. But a good conclusion does much more than simply close out your message. It can accomplish several important things for you.

First, it can reinforce what you have said. One good way to do this is to briefly summarize the main points you have made.

Put the whole communication into two or three short, but memorable, sentences.

Second, a good conclusion can invite people to act. It's like a salesperson asking for an order at the end of a sales presentation. To accomplish this, it must explain very clearly and precisely what action you desire, and be very convincing in its tone.

Third, in your conclusion, you can inspire your audience. You might leave them with a challenging question, a glowing promise, or a strong statement of your most compelling point. But make sure that your audience is inspired to do what you want them to do. Michigan's famous football coach, "Hurry-Up" Yost, once inspired his team with the conclusion of his half-time pep-talk to such a high level that they followed him out the wrong door—right into the swimming pool.

Fourth, you can set up future communications with a good conclusion. For example, you might end a letter with a statement like, "I look forward to a quick okay on this proposal, so that we may begin immediately to. . . ."

Develop a Good Outline

Think of your introduction, main body, and conclusion as a skeleton on which you can hang all of your information, ideas, arguments, and explanations. The analogy can help you to give your communications structure and shape, it can help you keep the various parts in perspective, and it can help you remember what you are going to say.

The head, or introduction, is the nerve center and primary sensing area. It contains mechanisms for seeing, hearing, tasting, feeling, and smelling—and it contains the brain which sends signals to every part of the body. A good introduction alerts as many of those senses as possible that something important is about to happen.

The trunk, or main body, contains the digestive system, the center of the emotions (at least metaphorically), and the connecting links for the appendages. Thus, the main body of the communication fulfills the promise of the introduction. It provides the substance of the hope excited by the introduction, gives a solid anchor for the embellishment of the appendages, and gives impetus to the legs and feet to carry out the desired action.

The *conclusion,* therefore, puts legs to the whole process. It carries the audience into the response you desire.

Let me illustrate how it all works by a brief letter:

Dear Mr. Smith:

Sally Brown, our mutual friend, asked me to tell you how she saved more than $1000.00 on a new car, and how you can, too.

She bought a new Pontiac, with all optional accessories, on our new "executive purchase plan," which was set up to meet the unique tax advantages of people like Sally—and you. It provides . . . which I'll be delighted to explain more completely when I see you.

I'll call you on Thursday morning to set up a time when you can see why Sally is so happy with her new Pontiac, and how you can cash in on your own savings. I look forward to meeting a person as astute as Sally told me you are.

Sincerely Yours,

Mary Jones

Mary Jones

Notice how the introduction sets up the subject of the letter. Assuming that Sally Brown is a close personal friend of Mr. Smith, using her name first is a strong grabber. The last clause draws Mr. Smith into the communication. The main body of the letter tells how Sally saved so much money, explains the plan Mary wishes to discuss with Mr. Smith, and implies that it will be to his advantage to spend some time listening to her when she calls on him. The conclusion summarizes the main body, makes a request, and sets up a future communication she hopes will take place.

TYING IT ALL TOGETHER

Targeted messages are concentrated messages which put power in your communications. The five steps to targeting are:

1. Target your subject—address the most compelling need of your audience.

2. Collect all the materials you need—gather all the explanatory and supportive information you need to prepare yourself and to use in communicating.
3. Select the materials you will use—choose the materials that best present your message.
4. Let the message ripen in your mind—take time to think about what you will say.
5. Organize your message into an outline—develop a clear introduction, a concise but complete main body, and a strong conclusion.

Even the simplest communications can be given with more impact when you follow these simple steps.

GROWTH EXERCISES

1. Study the main titles for at least five television shows. Make notes of how they gain and hold attention, introduce the subject, set the tone and mood for the show, introduce and get you to identify with the characters, compel you to watch them, and dispel any fears or anxieties you might have about watching.

2. Select three of your most successful recent communications and analyze them to see how they addressed the needs of your audience and your knowledge of the subject.

3. Look at the three messages you selected for exercise 2 and see how you organized them. Did they each have an introduction, a main body, and a strong conclusion? How might each of the parts of your outline been strengthened?

CHAPTER NINE

HOW TO TARGET YOUR PRESENTATION

Have you ever presented an idea or request that was soundly rejected? Or, equally frustrating, maybe you've made a presentation only to have nothing happen. In either case, what you proposed might have been great, it might have been targeted to the right audience, your approach might have been organized beautifully; but if your presentation did not produce the effect you desired it cannot be called effective communication.

The communications pros know that often what makes or breaks their best-laid plans is the way those plans are presented to their audiences. For them, the goal for every presentation is to get people to give them the response they desire without unnecessary delays. So they target every presentation to reach that goal.

A presentation is nothing more than a vehicle which you can use to convey your message. But, interestingly, it is often the greatest factor in determining what your audience hears, understands, and does in response to your message.

As we have seen, at least seventy percent of what we communicate in personal conversation is communicated through messages that are non-verbal. In other words, what we actually say accounts for less than one-third of what our partners in conversation receive from us. The remainder is transmitted through voice tone, expressions, and gestures.

Likewise, when we are speaking to a group of people—large or small—it is the way we speak and what we do that connects with our audience more than what we actually say. When our approach to an audience is through a medium such as broadcasting, videotape, or some form of written message, conveying the message we want to get across becomes an even tougher challenge. When you add the faulty receiving of messages by most people, the process of making a presentation convey the entire message you want to deliver requires careful thought, masterful delivery, and constant feedback to be even partially successful.

Many of the hazards of communication can be avoided by carefully targeting your presentations. Targeting means choosing the right medium to convey the message, using that medium to its maximum advantage, and targeting the response you desire. In this chapter, we will look closely at each.

CHOOSE THE RIGHT MEDIUM
FOR THE MESSAGE AND THE AUDIENCE

The communicator's choices of media are greater than ever. The communications revolution of recent years has opened up a tremendous number of options not previously available. The emphasis has shifted to "decentralization" of presentations through personalized media such as personal stereos and radios, personal computers, computer terminals at remote locations, videotape recorders, audio cassette players, etc.

As a result, it is now technically possible to reach audiences that were inaccessible a few years ago. Through satellite hookups, conference telephone calls, and videophones it's possible for us to hold meetings with several people in widely scattered locations.

Yet those of us who make our living as communicators are discovering that what is technically easier is actually becoming harder than ever. Part of the problem stems from the fact that competition for the attention of our audiences has increased dramatically with all the new innovations. For example, the friendly conversations that were so much a part of the jogging scene a few years ago are giving way to personal stereos. People who would often strike up conversations with others jogging along with them are now wearing headphones as they jog; and the most you can get out of them is a smile and a wave of the hand.

Another part of the problem many people are having making presentations in the new communications environment comes from their not understanding how to select the right medium to convey their messages. They're a little like the fox in one of *Aesop's Fables* who was boasting to a cat about all his clever devices for escaping his enemies. "I have a whole bag of tricks," he said, "which contains a hundred ways of escaping my enemies." Asked how many ways he knew, the cat replied, "I have only one, but I can generally manage with that." Suddenly they were attacked by a pack of hounds and the cat scampered up a nearby tree. "This is my plan," said the cat. "What are you going to do?" While the fox sat debating which escape to choose, the hounds overtook him and he was killed. Aesop's cat concluded, "Better one safe way than a hundred on which you cannot reckon."

Gadgets, gimmicks, and innovations can be useful in conveying messages, but many would-be communicators get so caught up in them that their media become their messages. They might get a lot of attention, but they do little with that attention. As communicators, our goal is to get a desired response from a targeted audience. *Remember, a presentation is only a vehicle to be used to convey your message.*

A few years ago, a large corporation spent a half-million dollars putting together one brief multi-media presentation. Staged with all the glamour of a Hollywood production, the presentation overwhelmed the audience, and the audience agreed to the proposal which the production put forth. Intrigued by the report of the presentation's success, I decided to follow up on it later to determine its long-range success. I discovered that, while the audience had initially agreed to the proposal, they had later done nothing to accomplish the desired actions. A year later, they felt they had been manipulated into a hasty decision, and highly resented it.

At the opposite end of the spectrum are the people who continue using a medium that is no longer reaching their audience effectively—just because it's convenient, or it's the way they've always done it. For example, a newsletter can be a valuable means of staying touch with an audience on a consistent basis, but if that newsletter is seldom read, it is foolish to rely upon it to convey important messages.

THE PRESENTATION REPRESENTS YOU

A survey which was done by the Rockefeller Foundation and published in *U.S. News & World Report* recently indicated that sixty-eight percent of customers who had quit buying from their regular suppliers did so because of the attitude their suppliers reflected to them through their communications—and lack of communication.

The person who answers the telephone for a company, or the salesperson who represents that company in the field, or the ad a company runs in the mass media becomes that company in the eyes of its customers. Everything any one of them does, or says, to the customer represents the company and helps to shape the customer's attitude toward it.

Likewise, every presentation you make *becomes* you to the audience which receives it—or fails to receive it. For example, when you write a letter, everything about that letter communicates something to the person who receives it. That person forms opinions about you from your letterhead, from the style and legibility of the type you use, from the grammar and spelling you use, from the tone of your wording—literally everything about that letter becomes you to the reader.

Choosing the right medium for your presentation, then, is a little like deciding which clothes to wear for a special occasion. There are certain criteria that must be used to choose which medium is most suitable.

CRITERIA FOR CHOOSING MEDIA

1. The medium you choose for your presentation must fit the image you wish to project.

It must be consistent with the way you see yourself and the way you want to be seen by your audience.

A suitable medium for your presentation will reflect your personality or the image you want your organization to reflect. For example, the chairman of the board of a large corporation would not choose a comic book format for his or her annual report to stockholders. Such a person would select a format that would reflect responsible management, creative leadership, and fiscal integrity.

To get a better idea as to how effective communicators convey their images through presentations, browse through various magazines and look at the ads they contain. Notice which companies appear in which magazines, what messages they seek to convey to the audiences that read those magazines and the personalities reflected by the way the companies advertise.

When you are choosing a medium to convey your message, choose the medium that best reflects the image you wish to project.

2. The medium you choose must also fit the audience you seek to reach.

It must be accessible, attractive, and attuned to the needs and interests of that audience. That's why it is so important to be aware of and sensitive to your audience. Choosing the right medium involves knowing what they read, how they relate to visual messages, how effectively you can reach them by telephone, what kinds of mail they receive, and a host of other important considerations. It is important to understand how your audience receives messages, and it is equally important to understand how that audience relates to you. There are certain media that you can use effectively with certain audiences because of the unique relationship you have with them.

For example, you can call a friend and chat about something that's on your mind. But try to call up a busy executive just to get to know the person better, and you'll have a tough job getting through—at least the second time.

The medium you choose to convey your message must be appropriate to the audience you wish to reach with that message. The more receptive they are to an approach through a medium, the better the chances you can use it to get through to them with your message.

3. The medium must fit your purpose for sending the message.

A medium that is attractive because it is convenient, economical, and simple might not be the best medium for conveying a message you consider important.

For example, a form letter asking for a donation from a mass audience might be quite acceptable if you are asking for, or expecting, small donations. But if you hope to receive a donation of $10,000, a form letter is not likely to accomplish your purpose.

In choosing a medium there are many considerations that will be determined by the purpose of your message. Cost, simplicity of preparation, plans for follow-up, and many other factors must be considered.

Probably the most important consideration in choosing a medium for your presentation is what kind of response you want it to produce. Effective communicators know that the medium must fit the purpose of sending the message, so they give careful attention to choosing the medium that best accomplishes their goal.

4. The medium must fit your message.

An expensive, elaborately printed brochure is probably not the best vehicle to use in communicating a decision to cut back on wage increases, or telling stockholders there will be no dividends forthcoming. Likewise, an ad in *Mad Magazine* is not likely to sell many Rolls-Royces.

The content and import of a message must always influence your choice of media for presenting that message. How complex is the message? What's the tone and nature of the message? What will the medium say about the message? These and many other factors must influence your choice of medium if you expect your presentation to have its desired effect.

5. The medium must fit the occasion.

Many years ago, a barber attended an old-fashioned revival meeting and responded to a "hell-fire and damnation" sermon. In his new-found zeal, he decided to share his new religion with his customers. The owner of the shop noticed the next day that something strange was going on. He watched as several customers came in for a shave and sat down in the chair. The new convert would lather them up, stroke his straight razor on the strap a few times, and lean over and softly say something to them. Quickly, they would jump up, tear away the apron, and dash out the door fully lathered.

"What are you saying to those customers?" asked the owner.

"I don't understand it!" replied the zealous barber. "All I said to them was 'Prepare to meet thy God!' "

It was clear that his medium didn't fit the occasion.

Few of us would be that insensitive, yet we often choose the wrong medium for the occasion. I've seen meeting planners schedule long audiovisual presentations on complex subjects early in the morning after all of the conventioners have been partying all night, or after they've just eaten a sumptuous meal at a luncheon. When the lights are turned up after the presentations, the audience has to be awakened.

The right medium for a presentation is the medium that will convey most effectively the message at the time it is sent to the audience. The mood of the audience, the tempo of the presentation, the nature of the occasion, what the audience will be doing at the time the presentation is given are all major considerations in choosing the right medium for the occasion.

6. The medium must have the capacity to convey the message you wish to present.

Just as you don't hunt a lion with a slingshot—unless your name happens to be David—you don't rely on an inadequate medium to convey a complex or important message.

Sending a photocopied one-page resume to a prospective employer for a job that pays $75,000 annual salary is not only a waste of money and effort, it closes off an opportunity to be considered for a position for which you might be qualified. Professional employment counselors suggest that you submit a resume that has the capacity to convey your capabilities to a prospective employer. Remember, that resume becomes you to a person who has never seen you.

A client once asked one of my associates to advise him on how to reduce the number of semi-skilled workers who left his company for other jobs—often for as little as a dime an hour more than they were making. "They often take benefit packages that are worth much less than what they have here," he said.

"But, do they know that?" the consultant asked.

"Sure," he replied. "We give them a booklet which explains it all as soon as they are hired."

Upon checking further, the consultant found that few of the

employees working for the company had ever read the booklet, and even fewer had understood what they had read. The booklet simply did not have the capacity to adequately convey the complicated message about benefits. The result was loss of good people and high costs of recruiting and training replacements for them. When a more adequate vehicle for conveying the message was developed, the turnover rate dropped substantially.

For the effective communicator, it is never enough to say, "I told them" or "I explained that to you." The pros have learned to choose a medium with the capacity to convey the message, and to check to see that the message has been properly received.

USING CRITERIA
TO SELECT THE MEDIUM

I have given you some of the criteria that I use in selecting the right medium for each presentation. However, the list is by no means exhaustive. By using my list as a guide, you might be able to develop a list of criteria that are tailored to your specific needs. The important thing is that you give careful attention to choosing the right medium to convey your messages for maximum effect. It is better to use a few media that you can use well than to waste valuable, and sometimes crucial, opportunities to convey your messages.

USE THE CHOSEN MEDIUM
TO MAXIMUM BENEFIT

Once you have chosen the medium you feel will best present your message, the next task is to take full advantage of the medium you have chosen.

Each medium has its own unique personality, its strengths, and its limitations. By tailoring your presentation to fit the capabilities of the chosen medium you can take advantage of its strengths and overcome its weaknesses. The more you study the medium you have selected, the better equipped you will be to tailor your presentation to take advantage of its power to convey your message.

Let me clarify that by an example. Let's say you have chosen to deliver your message to an audience through the medium of a speech. In chapter fourteen I'll give you some pointers on how to make a speech that gets response, but here I want us to focus on the unique personality of public speaking as a medium of conveying a message.

As president of the National Speakers Association, an organization serving the leading professional speakers in America, I can tell you that giving a speech is a widely used medium of communication for almost every area of human enterprise. The fact that public speaking is so commonly used is a strong indication that it can be a very effective way of conveying messages. But public speaking also has some definite limitations.

STRENGTHS OF THE SPEECH

Here are a few of the more obvious strengths of a public speech:

1. It is flexible enough to fit into a wide variety of formats and to convey messages on almost any subject.
2. A speech allows you to bring to bear the full power of your personality in making the presentation.
3. A speech's simple structure permits your message to be timely in adjusting to changing conditions and last minute changes.
4. It identifies you as a leader.
5. A speech puts you in touch with many people simultaneously and saves you unnecessary duplication of effort in telling individuals one at a time. The assembling of a group for a speech can also serve to unify that group.
6. The medium of public speaking allows for immediate feedback to indicate to you how your message has been received.
7. A speech opens the door to follow up with other forms of communication.

LIMITATIONS OF THE SPEECH

But there are some definite limitations to the capabilities of the speech:

1. There are definite limits to the number and complexity of the messages that can be delivered effectively through a speech.
2. Most people tend to remember more about the feeling a speech creates than they do about the content of the message it delivers.
3. Spontaneous feedback is often not as valid as feedback that comes after the message has been thought over carefully by the audience.
4. In a speech, you only get one shot. If that attempt to deliver the mes-

sage fails it is hard to salvage the message you want to convey.

5. A speech limits your contact with individual persons and it is sometimes difficult to see how key people are really receiving your messages.
6. A speech is vulnerable to competition from distractions and resistance from the audience.
7. Some people simply tune out any speaker because they have heard so many bad speeches.

WORK WITH THE STRENGTHS AND LIMITS

By understanding the strengths of a medium of communication you can take full advantage of all the capabilities of that medium. Chapters 11–17 of this book are devoted to the ways you can cash in on the strengths of a variety of media that are available to you for making your presentation. The more you study each vehicle for communication, the better equipped you are to make that medium work for you. Also, as you study the limitations of various media, you can develop strategies to overcome those weaknesses.

Remember, the presentation is a means of conveying your message, and a medium is only a vehicle for staging that presentation. Your purpose is to take full advantage of all the power a medium offers you in presenting your message.

TARGET YOUR PRESENTATION
FOR THE DESIRED RESPONSE

Regardless of the medium you choose, your goal for presenting a message is to get the response you desire. Your purpose is not simply to communicate, but to *communicate effectively.*

Here are some tips to help you target your presentations to achieve the response you desire.

TIP #1: BE SENSITIVE TO THE WAY YOUR AUDIENCE WILL EXPERIENCE THE PRESENTATION. Probably the most important thing you can do to put power into your presentation is to identify with the typical person who will be receiving that presentation. When you really understand how a person will relate to that presentation, you can tailor it to have its maximum impact.

For instance, I know that my clients are bombarded with paperwork and printed materials, so I try to handle as many details as I can in person or on the telephone. When it is necessary to send a client a proposal or some other document, I don't want it to get lost in the shuffle of papers, so I send it to the client by a commercial air express service. The cost is more than regular mail, but it gives the packet an aura of importance and urgency. It also ensures that it will be handed to the client personally. When he or she opens the packet, the recipient finds an attractive presentation and a request for immediate response. By being sensitive to the way they will experience my presentation, I can tailor it to have its maximum impact. Believe me, it works!

TIP #2: DON'T OVERLOAD YOUR PRESENTATION.   One of the most common reasons presentations fail to meet their objectives is that they try to accomplish too much. Thus, they end up accomplishing little or nothing.

Brochures, for example, can explain, or announce, or promote, or lend prestige, or remind, or serve as reference sources. In rare instances they can even sell. But almost never can you do all of those things in a single brochure. It is much more productive to select a few compatible functions for a brochure, and concentrate on doing those well, than to load the brochure with so many functions that it does none of them.

TIP #3: MAKE YOUR PRESENTATION ATTRACTIVE.   "A spoonful of sugar helps the medicine go down," says a song from *The Sound of Music.* That's a great thing to remember when you're putting together a presentation in any form.

Saving a few bucks on a printed piece might look attractive to you, but it often makes the presentation much less effective than it could be. Money spent on commercial art, color printing, enough paper to allow for a good layout, and tightly-written copy are usually well worth what they cost you. If you must hold down the cost, reduce the copy—not the presentation. The more readable a piece is, the better are your chances of getting your message across.

TIP #4: DEVELOP A STRONG SENSE OF TIMING.   A sense of timing is simply an awareness of how time affects every aspect of your presentation. It enables you to be in charge of the precise moment a presentation begins and ends, how long each part of it lasts, and the intervals at which communications take place.

You may think timing has only to do with oral presentations (and certainly it's an important consideration there), but it strongly influences almost any medium you choose for your presentation. One of my companies, for example, relies heavily on direct mail for its presentations to its customers. We notice constantly that our response is strongly affected by holidays, seasons, the day of the week a piece reaches a customer, and a host of other timing factors. We have to watch the schedules of our customers to make sure that our catalogs reach them at the precise moment they are most likely to be ordering the types of materials we sell. (Even the average length of time it takes a customer to read each piece of copy is controlled for maximum interest.)

Each medium of communication has its own timing factors, and every audience lives by its own schedule. A strong sense of timing can enable you to make time work for you, rather than against you, in all your presentations.

TIP # 5: CULTIVATE A SENSE OF PACING TO SUSTAIN INTEREST.   Pacing is controlling the intervals at which the various events within your presentation take place. Most audiences are rather fickle. Their attention spans are usually limited to two to three minutes. Whether they're reading something you've written or listening to something you're saying, they need a constant change of pace to keep their interest level high.

Notice, sometime, how your favorite radio station paces its programming format to keep you listening. Most records last about three minutes, because the music companies know that is about as long as a song will keep an audience. The hosts on radio shows will change pace constantly from one song to another. Even the commercials are paced for maximum interest level. As soon as one sound ends, another is there to keep you listening.

Professional speakers live by pacing their points, their stories, their pauses, their audience exercises, and their conclusions. Likewise, good writers use short paragraphs, many subheads, and other literary devices to lead readers along. A strong sense of pacing makes any presentation more interesting to its audience.

A good presentation sets up an audience to expect something important to take place. It's a way of taking charge of the communication situation. Staging is a way of putting a little show business into every presentation.

Staging can make all the difference in the world in how receptive an audience is to what you have to say. General Electric Company once invited me to speak at their National Sales Makers Convention in Honolulu. The setting was the beautiful Sheraton Waikiki Resort Hotel. Since these were the top salespeople in their company, they were treated like royalty. Every time they went to their rooms, they would find a little gift of some exotic food or nice wine. A musical group had been hired months in advance, and they had composed songs to give all the announcements. Everything the meeting planners did was designed to set a positive and upbeat mood. When I walked onto that stage to speak, that audience was thoroughly prepared to hear what I had to say.

Some novice communicators are reluctant to stage their presentations with flair and excitement for fear their audiences will feel manipulated. Of course, you can overdo it. But the real pros know that most audiences love staging and respond very positively to it.

Staging has become so much a part of the "American Way of Life" that most audiences expect it. Newspapers and magazines use headlines and strong layouts, television stages extravaganzas, radio heralds its announcements with musical lead-ins, direct mail houses use sweepstakes, stores use displays and lighting, and so on. If you want your message heard amid all the voices crying for attention, you simply must stage every presentation.

TYING IT ALL TOGETHER

How will you get your audience to give you the response you desire from your presentation? You can do it by targeting your presentation.

Targeting includes:

1. Choosing the medium of communication that best presents your message to the audience you wish to reach.

2. Using that medium to maximum advantage by playing to its strengths and compensating for its weaknesses.

3. Target the response you desire through careful selection of the messages you will send, by being aware of the way an audience will experience your presentation, by entertaining your audience, by timing for effect, by pacing to sustain interest, and by staging to set your audience to expect something important to take place.

However, you must keep it all in perspective. A presentation is only a vehicle you can use to convey your message. Everything about that presentation should be designed to convey the message with its desired impact and lead to the response you desire.

GROWTH EXERCISES

1. Think of an idea you have presented to an individual, or group, that was rejected. Using the suggestions of this chapter, analyze how you might have staged a better presentation of that idea, so that its chances of acceptance would have been greater.

2. Study your most recent presentations (oral, written, printed, etc.) to determine what they say about you to your audience. Do they truly project the way you want your audiences to see you, or the company you represent?

3. How aware are you of the strengths and weaknesses of the most common medium you use for presenting your messages? Select the medium you use most often (other than public speaking) and make a list of as many of its strengths and weaknesses as you can. Analyze how you can better utilize its strengths and compensate for its weaknesses.

4. Analyze how effectively you use timing, pacing, and staging in presenting your messages in your most common communications. How might you use them more effectively?

CHAPTER TEN

HOW TO TARGET YOUR RESULTS

"How was my first sermon, Granny?" asked the young minister. He knew she'd tell the truth.

"I saw only three things wrong with it," mused the frank old lady.

"Only three things wrong. . . . Not bad for my first attempt," said the young man excitedly. "What were they?" he asked.

"Wellll!" drawled the grandmother, "First, you read it! Second, you didn't read it well! And third, it wasn't worth reading anyhow!"

Few of us could stand much feedback like that. Nor is it likely to be very helpful.

In fact, the initial question the young man asked was aimed more at stroking his ego than at determining the results of his presentation. The real pros at communicating know that even their best efforts can be picked apart by critics, and that most people will simply pay them compliments when asked for an evaluation. For them, the appropriate question is: *Did my presentation produce the response I desired?*

Too many presentations are like the old line attributed to a doctor: "The operation was a success, but the patient died." Who cares if the operation succeeded if the patient died? Likewise, who cares if a speaker or writer makes a good presentation unless it produces the results that communicator had in mind? Novices look for noise, pros look for action. Amateurs feel that the worst failure is that an audience doesn't like a presentation, but seasoned communicators know that the worst failure is that nothing happens as a result of their presentation.

How will you know if the audience does what you want them to do? In this chapter, I will give you some tested and proven methods of obtaining and using the valuable feedback that can complete the communications cycle.

RESULTS ARE PROGRAMMED IN, OR THEY DON'T HAPPEN

One of the most common reasons audiences fail to respond to a presentation is that it was never made clear to them what response is desired. And the most common reason it is not made clear to the audience is that it is not clear to the communicator.

What if your audience did precisely what you wish them to do? What would that be, and how would you know that they did it? Before you answer those questions too quickly, let me illustrate what I mean. Let's say you have a great idea you want to present to the management of a group you represent. You present that idea in a speech you have carefully prepared and skillfully deliver. When you finish, the audience—to a person—compliments you with statements like "Brilliant speech!" and "Great idea!" However, a year later, you notice that nothing has been done to implement the idea.

If your goal was to make a good speech, it is clear that you have succeeded; but if your goal was to get the group to implement the idea, you'd have to say that you were less than successful. In other words, "The operation was a success, but the patient died."

Anyone who has a flair for showmanship can make a speech that will draw applause and compliments. But an effective communicator can give speeches that make things happen.

A salesperson on straight commission who only drew compliments would soon starve. What that salesperson wants is for people to buy.

TWO KINDS OF SUCCESS

There are two kinds of success that concern an effective communicator—short range success and long range success. Short range success has to do with the audience's understanding and relating positively to the actual presentation. Long range success comes when the presentation produces the ultimate effect the communicator desires. Both are important.

A group of investors once formed a franchise company and set about to sell franchises in certain areas of the country. Since the franchise they were selling was rather complex, they decided they would invite prospects to come to regional meetings where it would be carefully explained. They put together an excellent presentation that included visual aids, handouts, and question-and-answer sessions.

They were delighted when, after their first round of presentations, at least eighty percent of the people who attended said they would buy. All who indicated an interest were given two weeks to respond. At the end of the two-week period, the investors were dismayed that not one of the prospects had followed through. They began to check to see what had happened.

What they found was that, while the prospects had understood their proposal well enough to want to buy it, they had not understood it well enough to explain it satisfactorily to their accountants, lawyers, and spouses.

The investors had achieved short range success, but had failed to achieve long range success.

To correct the problem, the investors insisted that in all future meetings, each prospect would be required to bring his or her spouse and at least one advisor. By explaining their complex proposal to all persons involved in the buying decision, they were able to achieve long range success as well.

Effective communicators want their audiences to hear and understand their presentations, but they also want those audiences to give them the response they desire.

TWO KINDS OF FEEDBACK

To assure both long and short range success, you need two kinds of feedback: presentation feedback and message feedback. Presentation feedback tells you if your audience heard and understood what you presented, and message feedback tells you if they gave the response you desired.

The amount and nature of each kind of feedback will be determined by your goals for making a particular presentation. If, for example, you are testing several types of presentations to see which works best, you are probably more concerned with specific feedback on the presentations themselves. On the other hand, if you are testing the acceptability of an idea or product, your concern is more with the response the message produces.

A person who sells products through newspaper ads, for example, might want to know which newspapers draw the best response, or what wording draws best, or what issues of the paper draw best; or perhaps the concern is with the size or frequency of the ads. By devising a coded feedback system, that person can determine the most profitable way to advertise. Advertising agencies use complex structures to get this sort of feedback, but people who place their own ads often use simple devices like coupons with symbols on them or code letters in the box number to which the audience is invited to respond. The principle can be applied to a wide variety of communications situations.

Message feedback might be more important to a manager who has just explained a complex new system to a group of employees. A simple questionnaire might give a clear picture of how thoroughly the employees understand the system. As a supervisor, he or she could gain some valuable insights about how to make future explanations; but the primary concern is with making the system work. If the questionnaire reveals confusion about certain parts of the system, additional instructions can be given in those areas.

WATCH FOR SURPRISES

Alert communicators know that the type of feedback they go after can often reveal useful information of another type.

A dog food manufacturer once called in a group of experts to determine why a new product was not selling. It had been carefully developed to provide balanced nutrition, it contained all the flavors dogs like, and they were sure it was of the right consistency. But it was not selling!

They assumed that the problem must be either in their advertising or merchandising. Through interviews, they determined that the ads were pulling because people would buy one bag of it. They also discovered the price was right, and that most people were drawn to the packaging.

Finally, they stopped an old man in a store whom they had determined had previously bought a bag of the dog food and asked him a very unscientific question.

"Why didn't you buy again?" asked the interviewer.

"Welllll," drawled the old fellow, "my dog just don't like the darn stuff!"

The alert interviewer discovered that they'd been asking the wrong questions in their efforts to get feedback. Or maybe they'd been surveying the wrong audience. They might have learned more by asking the dogs.

Feedback that only strokes your ego or that only reinforces your biases is seldom very helpful. And often the attitude with which you evaluate the answers you get from it can determine how useful it is.

PLAN FEEDBACK *BEFORE* YOU MAKE YOUR PRESENTATION

How will you know if the audience gives you the response you desire? That question can help a great deal if it's asked before you make the presentation.

You might discover that the presentation you have planned simply does not have the power to give you the response you desire. You can, then, either develop a different presentation that does have the power or adjust your expectations to be more realistic. Or you might discover that portions of the presentation are weak in relation to the response you hope to get, and you can make adjustments to make them stronger.

In any case, it is better to spot weaknesses in presentations before they are given than to be disappointed later.

I have found it helpful early in the preparation stage to write out a succinct statement of what response I desire and to plan the feedback that will tell me if I have achieved that goal. That way, everything works together.

STRATEGIES FOR GETTING USEFUL FEEDBACK

There are several strategies that have been developed by skilled communicators over many years and have been proven successful.

STRATEGY #1: TEST YOUR PRESENTATION AND MESSAGE—NOT THE AUDIENCE. The real pros always assume the responsibility for communicating. It is a mark of an amateur to blame the audience for a failure—except in rare instances.

The teacher who gets angry with students because many of them do poorly on a test is more concerned about fixing the blame than fixing the problem. The skilled teacher knows that a test indicates a failure to stimulate enough interest in a subject, or a failure to present that subject effectively, or maybe even that the test itself was poor.

Of course, the best test of your effectiveness as a communicator is how much of your presentation your audience understood and how close they came to the response you desired. But that has more to do with your presentation and message than to how good an audience it was.

STRATEGY #2: TEST YOUR EFFECTIVENESS—NOT ABILITIES. Good feedback is not fishing for compliments. Asking people questions like, "Did you enjoy the presentation?" might produce glowing tributes, but it will not likely tell you anything truly useful. Specific questions that reveal what that audience understood you to say, and how they related to what you said, can be far more productive.

STRATEGY #3: LISTEN, OBSERVE, AND ASK QUESTIONS. Active listening and careful observation can often tell you more about how effective a presentation was than a formal approach reveals.

The host of a local television talk show once told me how he knew it was a hit, long before the ratings proved it. "When I was doing another show, people would come up to me and tell me they'd seen the show and enjoyed it. But after the first few shows in this new series people would stop me on the street to give me their opinions about the subjects we'd been discussing. There's all the difference in the world in the two kinds of response," he said.

When someone pays you a compliment, draw them out with questions to see if what they understood is what you meant. Observe the kinds of responses people give you.

STRATEGY #4: GIVE THE AUDIENCE SOMETHING SIMPLE TO DO IMMEDIATELY.   Make it clear that you are not evaluating them, but that you are interested in their opinions. "I've been telling you what I think, now I'd like to hear what you think about this subject," is a good way of introducing your request for feedback.

STRATEGY #5: DEVISE A WAY OF EVALUATING THE FEEDBACK YOU GET. Nobody is good enough to be successful with every person who hears every presentation he or she gives.

One way of evaluating is to quantify your responses. For example, direct mailers know that on certain types of mailers to certain types of audiences, they should get a response from two to five percent of the people who receive their mailer. When there is a money-back guarantee, they set an acceptable quota for the ratio of returns. When they get a higher response and a lower return rate than expected, they know they've been successful.

However, a person teaching children how to evacuate a building in case of fire cannot settle for less than total response. That person should keep getting feedback and making more presentations until every child knew exactly what to do.

STRATEGY #6: TAILOR YOUR FEEDBACK AND EVALUATIONS TO YOUR ULTIMATE GOALS.   A presentation might produce an immediate effect that is desirable, but might result in a long range problem for you. For example, you might sell an idea to one group, but in so doing, you could alienate another group that is equally vital to reaching your long range goals. An idea that thrills top management might be strongly resisted by the middle management people who will have to help you in implementing it.

FOLLOW UP ON FEEDBACK

Feedback only has value when it is put to good use. Good follow-up requires more than a casual glance through a few of the questionnaires your audience returns.

In fact, doing nothing about feedback can sometimes produce negative results. A supervisor who tells employees, "We want your input on management decisions," and then never does anything about the suggestions they make can expect those workers to question his or her sincerity.

TAKE FULL ADVANTAGE OF SUCCESS

If your feedback indicates that your presentation and message have been successful, make sure that you follow through to take advantage of all of the success.

It is far too easy to think of a good presentation as an end within itself—especially if it has taken a lot of work to put it together. But a successful presentation is often only the beginning.

For example, if your feedback indicates that you have staged a successful meeting which has produced some strong decisions, follow up to make sure those decisions are implemented. Or, if your short range feedback indicates that your audience has heard and understood what you have presented, make sure that you follow through to ensure that they give you the long range response you desire.

USE FEEDBACK TO BUILD
FUTURE SUCCESSES

One of the great benefits of making good presentations is that they open up new doors for future success. Don't let those opportunities slip through your fingers.

As a professional speaker, I never look at a presentation as a one-shot deal. Through what I call "vertical prospecting," I seek to turn every success into future successes. That way, I take full advantage of the momentum I have going with a group, and I also find other outlets for the presentations I have worked so hard to put together.

Let me illustrate. If an audience has been responsive to my presentation, I do two things immediately. First, I seek to book that group for another engagement, while the memory of that success is still fresh in their minds. Second, I look for individuals within that group with whom I can work on future projects. If I am speaking for a company, I keep my ears open for ideas as to how they can use my consulting services. If the group is sponsored by an association, I look for people within the group who can engage me for future engagements with other groups they work with, or can use my consulting services.

When a group responds positively to your presentation, don't simply pat yourself on the back and walk away. Take advantage of the opportunity to build future successes.

USE FEEDBACK
TO CORRECT MISTAKES

If your feedback indicates that your presentation was not as success-ful as you would have liked it to have been, take advantage of that feedback to learn how to do it better next time.

The novice crawls off from a failure and says, "I really blew it this time!" But the professional communicator asks, "Where did I go wrong?" That professional wants to know what to do dif-ferently next time to assure success. Through careful listening to feedback, you can correct your mistakes and do a better job next time.

LEARN WHAT WORKS BEST FOR YOU

The more experience you gain as a communicator, the less you are concerned with praise from presentations. The real question becomes, "What works best for me?"

When I take my automobile to my mechanic, he puts it on a diagnostic machine that tells him instantly what needs to be done to tune the car for maximum performance. His concern is not "Does it run?" but "How does it run best?"

Likewise, as a communicator, I am concerned with what works best for me in every situation. I listen and analyze my feedback so that I can fine tune every presentation to its maximum effective-ness. My goal is not to simply be good at what I do, but to be superb at it.

It is usually better to say, "I'll call you next week to discuss it further," than to tell someone, "Give me a call sometime and we'll talk about it." The reason: people get busy with other priorities and forget about following up with you.

When someone asks me for my business card after a talk, I usually don't give it to the person. I prefer to ask something like, "Was there something in particular that interested you?" If they say, "Yes" and tell me what it is, I will then say, "I'm often hard to reach by telephone; give me your business card and I'll see that you get the information you want." When I have obtained that person's card, I will write on the back of it the specific thing they are requesting and make sure that they get it. Then I will call the individual and see if they are satisfied. This personal attention often opens doors for future opportunities.

It is always easier to get through to a busy person when you are giving them the information they requested than it is to reopen a door they have closed.

TYING IT ALL TOGETHER

How will you know when your audience does what you want them to do? The best way to find out is through carefully designed feedback.

Good feedback does more than simply stroke your ego; it tells you how successful you have been in accomplishing your goals, how you have been successful, and what works and doesn't work.

Results are programmed in, or they don't happen. Feedback can tell you if you have obtained results—both in the short and long range. But good feedback only comes when it is planned before the presentation is given.

Feedback only has value when you carefully analyze what it means and follow up on it. You can use it to take full advantage of your success, to build future successes, to correct mistakes, to tell you what works best for you, and to fine tune your communications skills.

GROWTH EXERCISES

1. How do you know how successful your communications attempts are? Analyze the feedback strategies you use in your most common form of presentation. Do they test your presentation or your audience? Do they test your effectiveness, or do they simply test your abilities? Do you have an organized system of evaluating the findings you receive from feedback?

2. Earlier in the book I made the statement, "All effective communication is dialog." How do the statements in this chapter relate to that premise? Think of three ways you can use feedback to engage your most frequent audience in dialog through feedback.

CHAPTER ELEVEN

PERSONAL CONTACT: YOU ARE THE MESSAGE

Many people have called John F. Kennedy one of the most effective leaders in America's history—regardless of how they feel about his political positions. I agree!

I have carefully studied his private and public life, and several things have stood out as indicators. He demonstrated an ability to work with a wide variety of individuals, an ability to get people of widely differing viewpoints to work together, an ability to focus issues clearly, and an ability to inspire hope and stimulate action.

He was able to do all of that because he understood the power of dialog, and used it effectively in all his personal contacts. The reality in John Kennedy constantly connected with the reality in other persons in a way that, together, they could proceed to a new reality. In other words, he had the ability to get things done.

Study the lives of any of history's great leaders—the statesmen, the innovators, the agents of change—and you will discover they all used the power of personal contact to accomplish their goals. Not all of these individuals were understood, many of them were disliked, and some were even strongly resisted. But they all were able to get other people to do things through communicating with other individuals.

PERSONAL CONTACT IS YOUR STRONGEST VEHICLE FOR COMMUNICATION

Humans are born with a deep need to get into significant touch with other humans. The story is told of how infants in a pediatrics section of a major hospital were dying at a much higher rate than the general population. Various theories to explain the high death rate were explored by the hospital staff. They looked for possible infections, faulty procedures and practices, and other possible causes. But the babies kept dying at an alarming rate.

"I know why the babies is dying," an uneducated old orderly finally said to one of the staff doctors.

"Please tell us!" urged the doctor. "We'll listen to anything!"

"Well," she pointed out, "it ain't natural for babies not to be touched, to be held, to be talked to and sung to. These babies are separated from their mamas as soon as they are born, and nobody loves 'em."

Soon volunteers were brought in to hold the babies while they ate, to talk to them and touch them as they were being changed, and to simply cuddle and stroke them. The mortality rate dropped dramatically, almost instantly.

It is this need for getting into touch with other humans that draws us together, that makes us negotiate with each other, that enables us to work together, that causes us to seek company. And it is this need that puts the power in personal contact.

PERSONAL CONTACT REVEALS THE FULL REALITY OF *YOU*

When you meet someone who impresses you, what's the first thing you think. Most likely, it's "I'd like to get to know that person better."

Any professional salesperson will tell you that "eyeball to eyeball" contact beats any other form of communication ten-to-one. You can be most persuasive when the other person can look into your eyes, hear your voice, see your expressions, and feel your presence.

Perhaps that's one reason that sincere, honest, enthusiastic, and positive people make the best communicators. The better you get to know them, the more you like and trust them; and the more you are willing to listen to what they have to say.

PERSONAL CONTACT
CAN OVERCOME BARRIERS

A message that someone we love has been injured creates a strong desire to be with that person. We aren't satisfied with someone's account of how the person is getting along—we want to see for ourselves.

When we can contact other people personally, we can overcome the barriers that keep us from communicating effectively with them. We can deal with physical barriers like distance, distractions, and competition. And we can deal with the emotional barriers like biases, language differences, anxieties, images, and conflicting purposes.

Any skilled communicator knows it is easier to get people to pay attention to them when the contact is personal.

PERSONAL CONTACT ENABLES YOU
TO TARGET EFFECTIVELY

Specific attention enables us to target our audience—to zero-in on what reaches that person whom we want to reach.

Personal contact enables us to target our message to the specific interests, needs, and desires of the one individual who is listening to us.

Everything about our presentation can be tailored to appeal most directly to the individual who gives us an audience. Through personal contact, we can target the response we want from our message and presentation and to gain that response in smaller doses.

PERSONAL CONTACT ENABLES US
TO GET THE BEST FEEDBACK

When you are speaking to a large audience, it is often difficult to tell how much of what you are saying is getting through. But when you are talking to one person and listening to that person, you can tell instantly. Thus, you can adjust your presentation to the feedback you get.

In labor disputes, unions and management can write memos to each other, they can talk to the press, they can posture through actions; but the seasoned mediator knows that it is only when they sit down across the table from each other that meaningful negotiations can take place.

That's why the more skilled we are at listening, observing, asking questions, and reading gestures, the better we can become at personal contact.

WHY SO MANY COMMUNICATORS FAIL AT PERSONAL RELATIONSHIPS

Many people who are outstanding in the mass communications fields lead lives of conflict and disappointment on a personal level. Somehow they are not able to connect with the persons closest to them. Yet, it is personal relationships that most often enable us to get done the things that really matter to us, that make life worth living, and bring us most of our joy.

Why is it that so many outstanding business executives watch their families crumble around them? Why do so many excellent public speakers have difficulty getting along with people around them? Is it true, as some claim, that you can't be good in both the big arena and in the intimacy of personal relationships?

I think not, because too many great people have been thoroughly delightful to those closest to them. As the prison warden said to Cool Hand Luke, in the movie by that name, "What we've got here is a failure to communicate!"

Let's focus on some of the reasons that communication on a personal level tends to break down.

1. Relationships break down when there is a preoccupation with self. Self-centered people tend to monopolize the talking; secure people tend to monopolize the listening. Selfish people suffer from "agenda anxiety." They concern themselves only with what they want to say or to get done.

If you would be successful at personal communication, concern yourself with the needs, desires, and motivations of others.

A good conversationalist constantly looks the other person in the mind.

When it comes to effective communication on a personal level, the Golden Rule is as appropriate as it was 2,000 years ago.

2. Personal communication is hindered by hasty assumptions. The person who jumps to a conclusion, might find that it brings a conclusion to the conversation. Even if you win an argument over whose viewpoint is right, you might end up losing a friend. It's a little like the fellow who demanded the right-of-way on the highway. He was right—dead right!

The person who finishes another's sentences, denies another's right to a differing opinion, and approaches others with suspicion is destined to spend a great deal of time alone.

Remember, every person we meet is potentially either a friend or a foe; what makes the difference is our willingness to engage that person in dialog.

3. Personal contacts fail when we are negative. Nobody likes to be around a person who is always looking at the dark side of life. The person who constantly says such things as, "The glass is half-empty," or, "It won't work," is destined to go it alone.

I have a friend in Florida named Charlie, who is a perfect delight to be with. Ask him on Monday if he's having a good day, and he'll smile and say, "Today is the best day of my life!" Ask him on Tuesday, and it's still the best day of his life. The answer is the same on Thursday, Friday, or Saturday.

"Charlie," I once asked him, "how can today be the best day of your life every time I see you?"

"Nido," he said cheerily, "Yesterday is gone forever, tomorrow is not mine yet. Today is the only day I ever have, so that makes it the best day of my life!"

Now, Charlie did not say, "Don't plan for tomorrow." Nor did he say, memories mean nothing. What he said to me was, "Receive this day, with all of its wonderful gifts."

People enjoy being with positive people.

4. Personal contacts become strained when the desire to be liked overrides the desire to be respected. The person who tries

to be all things to all people ultimately fails to be what he or she could be to a few. But the person who tactfully takes a stand is respected and appreciated by others; even if they disagree with the stand.

A close personal friend of mine says, "It's our enemies from whom we learn the most." He explains it like this: "Most of us tend to operate on half-truths, and to surround ourselves with those who share those half-truths, but our enemies make us question what we believe. So we can learn from them."

Contrary to what some people think, dialog is hindered, rather than helped, by always saying "the right things." As someone said, "Conflict is the price we pay for growing intimacy."

5. Failure to practice good human relations hinders personal communication. Interrupting other people, putting down the opinions of others, ignoring the feelings of others, and constantly being late are examples of rudeness that can close off communication.

People who are courteous to all, regardless of station or position, usually find a ready audience for conversation. Managers who treat employees with dignity and respect usually get better cooperation. And people who remember names usually get those whose names they call to pay attention to them.

TIPS TO HELP YOU TOWARD BETTER PERSONAL COMMUNICATIONS

Here are some tips I've found very helpful in keeping the channels of communication open with other people.

1. Concentrate on making others like and enjoy *themselves*—they'll enjoy you more.
2. Give others the benefit of the doubt, and doubt often—emphasize the benefit.
3. Forget your ability to think faster than another person talks—everybody has it, but only the foolish use it. When you're thinking ahead, you can't hear what's being said.
4. Listen at least twice as much as you talk—others will hear twice as much of what you say.
5. Laugh *with* others often—only fools never laugh, or laugh *at* others.

6. Use plain talk—say what you mean, precisely what you mean, and only what you mean.

7. Ask for more advice than you give—the wise seek counsel, the foolish only give it.

8. Criticize sparingly, and then only constructively—one compliment is always worth a dozen critical remarks.

9. Be approachable—few people talk often to a dragon, or a stone wall, or a ghost.

10. Seek to know others—you'll be amazed at how it will help you understand yourself.

11. Greet every person you meet cheerfully and enthusiastically—nobody can fake cheerfulness and enthusiasm very long. You'll either quit trying or improve your outlook.

12. Leave every person feeling better for having talked to you—they'll be happy to see you next time.

ADD POWER TO YOUR PERSUASION

People who are persuasive can get things done; and they can do it without demanding, or ordering people around, or being manipulative. Here are some ideas that can help you become more persuasive in all your relationships and communicating:

1. Have you discovered the tremendous power of asking questions?

Would you like to get people more involved in what you are saying and doing? Have you noticed that people respond very warmly to the right kinds of questions? For example, don't you like it when someone asks you for your opinion about something? Or when they ask you what you'd like?

But isn't it frustrating when someone asks you several questions, then doesn't give you a chance to answer? Or isn't it worse when the person who asks pays no attention to what you say in response?

Skilled communicators know that asking questions can add power to their persuasion, so they ask a lot of questions. By asking questions you can discover what people want and gain what you want by helping them to get it.

Let's look at some of the many benefits from regularly asking questions:

1. Questions give you valuable information about what people are thinking, feeling, and understanding.
2. By asking a lot of questions, you can learn many things that will be useful to you.
3. When you ask questions, you show an interest in other people.
4. When you ask questions, you can draw the other person into the dialog—you can make them a part of the communications process.
5. Questions help you determine what misconceptions the person may have about you or what you are saying. That gives you an opportunity to clarify false impressions.
6. Questions also help you clarify misconceptions you may have about the person and what they are thinking.
7. Questions help you to focus issues, define problems, and frame options.

These are only a few of the many benefits you derive when you ask a lot of questions in your personal contacts. But they should be enough to let you know that questions contain tremendous persuasive power.

However, there are some cautions about asking questions:

1. Never ask nosey or very personal questions; they might offend the person.
2. Always allow a person to answer questions completely before responding. When you interrupt a person in mid-answer, the person feels manipulated.
3. Always listen carefully to the answers a person gives. Nothing makes you look less interested than failing to pay attention after you have asked a question.
4. Avoid questions about politics, religion, or other issues that could spark a heated discussion on things not related to what you want to talk about.
5. Frame questions so the person can give positive responses.
6. Avoid disagreeing with the answers a person gives to your questions. When you ask a question, then try to knock down the person's answer, he or she feels set-up.
7. Avoid making the person feel dumb or uninformed by the questions you ask or the way you frame them. When you ask a detailed question that the person logically does not know the answer to, and then you spout out the answer, you imply that the person is ignorant for not knowing something you know so well.

Skilled communicators add power to their persuasion by asking a lot of questions, by asking them tactfully, and by listening carefully to the responses people give.

2. Take control of your non-verbal signals. Studies have shown that people tend to believe your non-verbal messages more readily than they believe your verbal messages. When the non-verbal signals you send agree with the verbal messages you are sending, they make what you say more convincing. When they disagree, they detract from the credibility of your verbal messages.

For example, when you look out the window, or at your watch, and say, "I care about what you think," the person usually believes the visible show of lack of interest. Or when you twitch nervously while giving a controversial statement, the person tends to think you are lying.

What you do is often more important than what you say. Take charge of your non-verbal messages. Look other people squarely in the eyes, tailor your facial expressions to fit your remarks, and make your whole body a medium for sending the kinds of messages you wish to send.

Many a sale has been lost because the salesperson sent the wrong non-verbal message at precisely the wrong moment, and many an intense negotiation has failed because an expression or gesture betrayed the weakness in a bargaining position. If you would become more persuasive, study and use to good advantage every non-verbal signal available to you.

3. Prove what you claim. Just because you say something, don't expect everyone to accept it at face value; particularly if it is a controversial claim. To convince people you are right, you must establish your authority to make your claims.

Persuasive people back up what they say with strong supportive information, accepted facts, and convincing arguments. Of course it's important to be positive and enthusiastic about your claims; but it is equally important to let others in on why you are so positive and enthusiastic.

Now, more than ever, people are questioning the traditional authorities and institutions. For example, you need only to look at the wide variety of health food products on the market, the tremendous number of recent diet books, and the wide range of exercise programs available to see that long established claims about how to stay healthy are being questioned by millions of people. Look around you, and you will see evidence that this trend is reflected in almost every facet of our lives.

If you would be more persuasive, learn to back up everything you say with raw data, illustrations and examples, and supporting documents. Make your claims clear, and then make them credible by supporting them solidly. When you say, "You won't believe this, but . . . ," they probably won't. But if you practice saying things positively, then prove what you say, you can become much more convincing.

TYING IT ALL TOGETHER

Personal contact can be your strongest vehicle for communicating with other people. It reveals the full reality of you, it enables you to overcome barriers, it enables you to zero-in on the most precise audience, and it is your best audience for feedback.

Communication with other individuals fails most often when we are preoccupied with ourselves, when we make hasty assumptions, when we are negative, when we'd rather be liked than respected, and when we fail to practice good human relations.

Each of us brings to the bargaining table of life something that is of value to others, and each of us needs something others bring to that bargaining table. The only way to win in life's give and take is to make sure that everyone who negotiates with us wins.

GROWTH EXERCISES

1. Select the one person you enjoy most talking with and analyze why you enjoy that person above others. Are there things that person does that you could use to good advantage in reaching out to others?

2. Look carefully at your most recent breakdown in communication with a person close to you. In light of what has been said

in this chapter, how could you have been more successful in that attempt?

3. Make a copy of the list of tips for better personal communications from this chapter and post it where you can easily see it. Concentrate on a different one of them for each of the next twelve days. Keep working at them until you master them. It will put real power in your personal contacts.

CHAPTER TWELVE

YOUR TELEPHONE: TOOL OR TYRANT?

When Alexander Graham Bell invented the telephone he missed the target he was aiming for. He was actually trying to invent a hearing aid for his beloved wife, who was nearly deaf. Unfortunately for her, he invented the telephone instead.

Now there are many people who say that we are the ones who are unfortunate. For them, the telephone is a time-wasting tyrant. But there are many of us who have found it to be a very useful tool—a tool of communication that enables us to do things we simply could not otherwise do.

Whether your telephone is a tool or a tyrant depends on how effectively you use it to accomplish your goals. I want to give you a few pointers I have found useful in communicating via phone.

USE YOUR PHONE: DON'T LET IT USE YOU

There must be a pretty good reason that AT&T (the telephone company) has become one of the largest corporations in the world. In a free society, people tend to choose to spend their money on things that benefit them—not things they don't want.

Here are some tips to help you use your phone, rather than being used by it.

1. Don't jump every time it rings—unless your business demands it. You'll find it a more valuable tool if you control the time you devote to talking. If you have a secretary, let him or her take calls for you, then return those calls at a time you designate for that purpose. If you have no one to take calls, and it is imperative that certain people reach you by phone, there are several options. You can use a professional answering service or paging system that can screen your calls, or get an unlisted number and only give it to those people whose calls have priority, or—as a last resort—get an answering machine.

2. Organize your telephone time. Make a list of the important points you want to cover, cover them quickly, and terminate your calls as quickly as you can without being discourteous.

If you have to make a lot of calls, it might help to get an automatic dialer, which enables you to dial your most frequently used numbers with the push of a button. That saves you the time of looking up numbers. Otherwise, keep frequently called numbers handy and in order.

3. Use your phone to replace letters, whenever possible. A quick phone call can often eliminate the need for writing, or dictating, a letter. Make notes of what was said and keep them organized for ready reference.

4. Use your telephone to replace personal visits, whenever possible. Visits to and by other people eat up much more time than phone calls. Unless your personal presence is a necessity, stay in touch by telephone. That way you can save travel costs, valuable time, and get in touch with more people more often.

5. Use conference calls to eliminate meetings, where feasible. Many meetings can be eliminated by a quick conference call. That can save everybody involved a great deal of time and money.

PUT POWER IN YOUR PHONE USAGE

There are ways you can increase your effectiveness on the telephone to accomplish your goals and to enable the real person you are to come through.

1. Go for the goal. When you communicate with another person by phone, there are basically four things you want to accomplish:

1. You want to be heard and understood. You want the other person to know exactly what you mean.
2. You want to be accepted. You want to get people to agree with you; or at least give you a sympathetic ear.
3. You want to get something done. You want people to understand what you want done, why it should be done, when (and sometimes how) it should be done—and you want them to act.
4. You want to understand others. You want to know how they feel about you, about the situation you're discussing, and perhaps about other things.

As you concentrate on these four objectives, you can apply them to each telephone call. This enables you to develop strategies to meet each objective and to reach your goal for the call. Structuring calls around these objectives enables you to put power in your phone usage.

2. Let your real personality come through your voice. On the phone, your voice is the only communication tool you have. Make it count in the following ways:

1. *Stay alert.* Alertness is hard to fake. Sit up straight, pay attention, and respond immediately to what is being said.
2. *Be pleasant.* Smile, even though the other person can't see you. A smile shows up in your voice. A cheerful voice can overcome the barrier of distance.
3. *Be natural.* Use simple, straightforward language and expressions. Talk just as you would in the presence of the person.
4. *Be distinct.* Speak clearly and distinctly, with your mouth open so the sound can come out. Talk directly into the transmitter. Don't shout; you'll blast the other person's ears off. A normal tone of voice is best.
5. *Be expressive.* Vary the tone of your voice. Talk at a moderate rate. Add extra expression to compensate for the person not seeing your face. But don't overdo it.
6. *Be sincere.* Know what you're going to say, but don't read it. Say only what you know to be true, and say it as if you really mean it.
7. *Be discreet.* Many expressions that are persuasive in person become offensive when filtered through the phone. Don't be timid, but since

you can't watch the person's face, watch what you say and how you say it.

PRACTICE GOOD TELEPHONE MANNERS AND TECHNIQUES

Just as you wouldn't make an important visit in sloppy clothes, with hair disheveled, and with a bad case of body odor, you need to watch your manners over the telephone. First, let's look at some ways of being courteous over the phone, and then I'll list some dos and don'ts for phone usage.

1. Be Courteous Over the Phone.

- *Answer Promptly.* When you keep people hanging on a long time, it's like saying, "Your time is not as valuable as mine!" Remember, the time seems much longer to the person waiting than it does to you.
- *Identify yourself.* A telephone transmitter alters your voice enough to make it hard for people to recognize it immediately. Whether you are calling, or being called, clearly identify yourself first thing.
- *Be warm and friendly.* The other person can't see your warmth, so you have to put it into your voice and into the expressions you use.
- *Be ready.* Keep a pencil and paper handy to take down any information the person wants to give you. Nothing sounds sloppier than saying, "Wait a minute while I get a pencil and paper."
- *Don't interrupt, but be interruptible.* Let the person finish before you have your say. Yield to the other person at the slightest indication he or she wants to talk.
- *Sign off warmly.* Take time to be gracious. Say thank you, or whatever is appropriate. Take the phone from your ear only when you are sure the other person has said his or her last word.
- *Hang up gently.* Slamming the receiver in the ear of a listener is even more offensive than slamming a door in that person's face. It's a good idea to let the other person hang up first. Gently lay the phone in its carriage.
- *Be discreet.* When you're off the phone, make sure you're really off. Laying an open receiver on your desk is like bugging your whole office. Likewise, holding the transmitter away from your mouth, even with your hand over it, can allow everything you say to come through. Make sure the person hears only what you intend.

149

2. Some "Do's and Don'ts" for Telephone Usage:

DON'T	DO
1. Frown	1. Smile
2. Mutter	2. Speak clearly and distinctly
3. Sound tired	3. Be enthusiastic
4. Speak in a monotonous tone	4. Lower the pitch of your voice for friendly conversation
5. Be negative	5. Talk in positive mood
6. Be overconfident	6. Be prepared to answer questions
7. Talk down into transmitter	7. Talk directly into mouthpiece
8. Ramble	8. Come to the point; ask for what you want
9. Do something *to* the listener	9. Something *for* the listener
10. Argue	10. Discuss
11. Hang up abruptly if request is refused	11. Politely thank person for listening to you

TYING IT ALL TOGETHER

Your telephone can be a tyrant that interrupts you, wastes your time, and damages your relationships. Or it can be a useful tool that can save you time and money, work for you, and enable you to do things that are impossible otherwise.

The key question is: "Do you use your phone, or do you let it use you?"

GROWTH EXERCISE

Rate yourself on a scale of 1 [low rating] to 5 [high rating] on each of the following questions:

1. How quickly do you answer your extension?
2. How do you identify yourself? your department? your company?
3. Is the response to the caller's opening statement appropriate?
4. Do you interrupt the caller or fail to give way when the caller tries to interrupt?

5. If the call is suspended, do you leave the line and return to the line in a polite manner?

6. Are you attentive to the caller's statements or do you ask questions which indicate you were not listening?

7. Do you express appreciation, concern, or regret where it is appropriate to do so? Do you apologize, if necessary?

8. Do you express in words, or indicate by manner and tone of voice a willingness to be of help?

9. Is your attitude friendly, helpful, and interested, or does the caller receive routine treatment instead of individual consideration?

10. When the nature of the contact requires that you provide information or explanation, is it given completely and concisely?

11. Do you use technical terms, slang, or arbitrary phrases?

12. Do you handle calls in a manner that would inspire confidence in the way your company is managed? Will the caller want to remain a customer?

13. Are the final arrangements clear?

14. Do you respond appropriately to the caller's "thank you," or other closing remarks?

15. Do you transfer calls thoughtfully? Do you return to the line every 30 seconds if there is no pick-up?

16. Do you plan your calls ahead?

17. Do you always listen for the dial tone before dialing?

18. Do you keep paper and pencil handy?

19. Do you hang up receiver gently and securely?

20. Do you wait for the other party to hang up the receiver first?

SCORING: Total up your rating points: 90–100, Good; 80–89, Fair; 70–79, Needs Improvement; below 70, Poor.

CHAPTER THIRTEEN

HOW TO HOLD MEETINGS LIKE THE PROS

Many busy people avoid meetings like a disease: they feel meetings are a waste of valuable time. Others look at meetings as a status-symbol. For them, it matters little what the meetings accomplish; what matters is that they attend a lot of meetings, and that the right people know they are in demand for meetings.

But the pros know that meetings can be very useful in exchanging ideas, information, and opinions. They know that meetings have the potential for bringing together people with varied backgrounds who can contribute something of value to the dialog.

The pros count on meetings to get things done; but they also know that productive meetings don't just happen. Good meetings are the result of careful planning and preparation, skillful leadership, and thorough follow-up.

In this chapter, I want to focus on how you can get the most out of meetings as a vehicle for communicating.

PLANNING AND PREPARATION DETERMINE SUCCESS OR FAILURE

In my work as a speaker and consultant, I lead or contribute to more than 250 meetings each year, and I can tell you that the difference in whether those meetings succeed or fail is determined by how carefully they were planned and how well the leaders and those who attend are prepared for them. In other words, the success or failure of a meeting can usually be predicted *before the meeting begins*. Most meetings that are productive are carefully planned.

When someone says, "Let's get our heads together and see what we can come up with," those who attend this kind of meeting can usually count on coming up with a headache—and little more.

Think for a moment about some of the meetings you have attended. Did you find them stimulating, enjoyable, and productive? Did you come away feeling that the time you spent in the meetings was well spent?

Now, think about how the meetings you feel positive about were led. How and when were you notified to attend them? Were you adequately prepared? Or did you get called in at the last minute, and wonder what the meeting was all about? Did it look like the leader had his or her act together?

If you want to ensure that the meetings you conduct are interesting, inspirational, and productive, learn to ask the right questions as soon as you know you're going to lead them. Here are some questions I have found very helpful in preparing for meetings, and some ideas on each of them:

1. *Is this meeting really necessary?* If so, why? Calling a meeting because we're supposed to get together every Monday is seldom a good reason for pulling talented, productive people away from their tasks. If you can get the job done without holding a meeting, then calling a meeting is a waste of time for you—and all who attend it.

2. *What is the purpose of this meeting?* There are basically four types of meetings that are commonly held:

- Information gathering meetings
- Information giving meetings
- Motivational meetings
- Idea-exchange and problem-solving meetings.

Sometimes you can do a little of each of the above things; but, usually, it is more productive to stick primarily to one purpose. A clear, concise statement of the purpose of a meeting is often your most valuable preparation.

3. *What is the goal of this meeting?* Ask yourself, "If the meeting were already over, what positive changes would I like to see as a

result?" Be specific. If it's information you want, what information? If it's ideas, what kinds of ideas, and on what? If you want to give information, what information do you want to give, and what do you want the participants to do with it? If you want to motivate them, what do you want to inspire them to do? What problems will you seek to solve?

4. *Who should attend this meeting?* There should be a clear reason as to why each person has been asked to attend. Selecting the people who can deal with the issues to be raised, and eliminating the people who are not really needed, might prove one of the greatest tests of your leadership ability.

5. *Who should conduct this meeting?* Often the person who is willing—or the person who is "drafted"—is not the best person to lead a meeting. Knowing when you should conduct a meeting, or when you should ask another person to lead it, can make the difference between success or failure. Why should the person being chosen be selected to lead the meeting?

6. *What procedures and rules will govern the meeting?* Parliamentary procedure has been widely used by groups because it provides a framework in which much work can get done. Other groups prefer a less formal approach. The important thing is that you have a procedure in mind, and that everyone is informed of that procedure. People who say, "We'll just talk about it until we reach an agreement," almost never reach that agreement—at the least, they waste a lot of valuable time.

7. *Where should the meeting be held?* A rule that has been especially helpful to me is to choose the most productive setting. The room should have minimal distractions and few possibilities for interruptions. It should be comfortable—but not too comfortable—and have available all the resources you need to accomplish your goals.

8. *What information should be sent to participants before the meeting?* Also, what information should be given out at the meeting? A meeting that starts out with a statement like, "Take a few minutes to look over the budget and see if you have any questions," will usually be a time-waster. Participants should be briefed as fully as necessary for them to come to the meeting ready to act on the issues raised. Information given out at the meeting should be explanatory, and should relate primarily to follow-up. The less reading people have to do during a meeting, the better.

9. *What audiovisuals do we really need for this meeting, and who should prepare and present them?* The right audiovisuals, properly prepared and effectively presented, can facilitate action in a meeting. They can be very helpful in explaining complex information and ideas. However, if they are thrown together hastily and are fumbled through, they detract more than they add. Make sure that they are ready, and that the person presenting them knows what to do.

10. *When should the meeting begin and end?* Meetings that begin late and drag on for hours after the issues have been effectively dealt with waste time and usually leave participants frustrated. Also, meetings that end abruptly because too much time was wasted getting started and dealing with minor issues cause ill feelings. Include only those items on the agenda that really need action at the time of the meeting, start on time, and end when you promised you'd end.

By asking these ten questions, and carefully planning around them, you can turn meetings into enjoyable, inspiring, and productive vehicles for communicating.

PROVIDE STRONG LEADERSHIP DURING THE MEETING

"A camel is a horse put together by a committee" is an old saying that too often rings true. And, sometimes, the bigger the committee, and the longer the meeting, the less like a horse the end product looks.

The surest way to avoid the too-many-cooks-spoil-the-broth problem is to provide strong leadership during the meeting. This does not imply that the chairperson must rule with an iron hand. What it means is that someone should lead the assembled group toward their goals.

When the purpose of a meeting is to give out and explain information, it is a good idea to take firm control of every facet of the meeting.

However, when meetings are called to gather information, solve problems, or take advantage of opportunities, maximum participation from all who attend is highly desirable. Here are some tips that can help you do that:

First of all, clarify the problem (or problems) and motivate the group properly. Understanding what the real problem is—not assuming that it is what it seems to be—is the first step in solving that problem.

To begin with, you should state what the problem appears to be. Next, you might ask for clarifications as to the true nature of the problem. Remember, your goal is to fix the problem—not the blame. Then, you should select the final agenda based on the real problem(s). Second, list all reasonable solutions and explore options. Third, choose a course of action. Fourth, assign responsibilities for implementing the solutions. Fifth, set deadlines and follow-up procedures for all assignments. Finally, adjourn. Quit while you're ahead.

LEARN HOW TO KEEP THE MEETING FROM GETTING OUT OF HAND

Here are some situations that can arise in meetings and some suggestions for handling them:

- *SITUATION: The group breaks up into private conversations.* Often, when emotions are stirred by controversial issues or actions, people will begin talking among themselves about the issues or actions. You'll appear inept if you let it continue.

To handle this situation, you should ask the speaker to stop until order is restored. Then you should call the group to order and ask the talkers to share their comments with the entire group, in turn and in an orderly fashion. But if the problem persists, call the talkers by name and ask them to join the group. As a last resort, ask uncooperative people to leave. Keep cool and be tactful at all times—whatever happens.

- *SITUATION: Someone tries to take over the meeting.* Extroverts have a way of showing up at meetings and trying to take over. If you know a person to be prone to do this, give him or her a seat next to you and try to control through whispers. If possible, give that person a role in the meeting that satisfies the need to be heard. If the takeover attempt becomes too overt, impose a rigid rule as to when each person may speak.

- *SITUATION: Some people won't say anything.* Try to involve them in the discussion by asking them a specific question. Draw them out by follow-up questions. Assure them their opinions are valid and welcomed.

- *SITUATION: You have uninvited guests.* If it is an open meeting, or the individuals are welcome, acknowledge their presence and invite them into the discussion. Otherwise, very politely (preferably privately) ask them to leave.

- *SITUATION: There are late arrivals.* Always arrange the room so that the door is to the rear, and leave extra seats near the door. Ignore their coming in.

- *SITUATION: People are distracted.* Arrange in advance for a room that is at a moderate temperature (a little cool is best because body heat raises the temperature), has few distractions (outside windows, etc.) and is properly lighted (too much is better than not enough). Select chairs that are comfortable (but not too comfortable). Make sure everyone can see and hear you as well as other program participants, and all audiovisuals. Most people enjoy attending good meetings on issues that matter to them. As a communicator, you can make sure that those who attend find your meeting both pleasant and productive. Remember, they are looking to you to take charge.

GOOD FOLLOW-UP
ASSURES GOOD MEETINGS

A meeting is productive *only* if the decisions reached result in concrete and positive actions that lead to the desired goal. The most common failure of meetings is that, when they are over, nothing happens.

You can avoid wasted time and missed opportunities resulting from meetings that get nothing done, if you will follow these suggestions: First, make sure everyone understands his or her assignments. Second, distribute minutes from the meeting as soon as possible. Third, assist all participants with their individual assignments. Fourth, check to see that all deadlines are met. Fifth, plan follow-up meetings when they are needed.

Good meetings don't just happen. They are carefully planned, skillfully led, and thoroughly followed up. As a communicator, you are expected to help people work together through meetings. Those who do it well experience the rewards of sharing constant growth and progress with those around them.

Remember, people willingly attend meetings when they expect something worthwhile to take place, feel they are needed, and are treated with dignity and respect. Don't forget to publicly thank everyone who contributes to making your meeting a success.

GROWTH EXERCISE

Using the guidelines in this chapter, evaluate a recent meeting you have attended. How could the meeting and its participants have been better prepared in advance? How effectively did the person in charge of the meeting lead the meeting? How might the meeting have been more productive? What follow-up would have given the meeting greater success?

CHAPTER FOURTEEN

PUT POWER
IN YOUR SPEECH

There are three kinds of speeches you can make:

- *Impromptu*—where you're called on to make a speech with no time for preparation.
- *Extemporaneous*—where you ad-lib a speech you have carefully prepared.
- *Written Text*—where you write out every word and read it before an audience.

Now, since people who are good enough to make a powerful impromptu speech probably won't read this anyway, we won't talk about that kind. And, since Richard Burton and the dozen other people who can convincingly read a written text probably don't need much help either, we'll talk about the other kind—the kind most of us mortals can give, and want to be able to give better.

If it's true that the pen is mightier than the sword, then it's equally true that a good extemporaneous speech is more powerful than a nuclear bomb.

Maybe you're not out to keep the world from being blown apart, or to change the course of history. Maybe you just want to be able to speak to the PTA chapter, or a group of business associates, or a convention audience—without either looking like a dunce or dying of cardiac arrest. Perhaps you'd even like to get people to pay attention to you, and to do something that matters a great deal.

Your skills as a speaker can be greatly improved as you learn to answer ten questions about each speech—the way the pros do it. I'll give you some clues as to how to answer these questions most effectively. Also, I'll give you some pointers that can help you put your personality to work in front of a group.

QUESTION #1: WHY SHOULD I SPEAK TO THIS AUDIENCE, IN THIS PLACE, AT THIS TIME?

1. Because I have some valuable information or insights I want to give this group.
2. Now is an appropriate time, and this is an appropriate place to share it.
3. This audience will accept my leadership—provided I earn it when I speak.
4. I have something important I want this audience to do.
5. Someone must believe I am the appropriate speaker because they invited me.

QUESTION #2: WHAT SHOULD I SPEAK ABOUT?

1. I should speak about something I know about, or can find out about.
2. I should speak about something of vital interest to me—something I can get really excited about.
3. I should speak about something the audience knows at least a little about—something they want to know more about.
4. I should speak about something that is timely and appropriate for this audience.
5. I should stick to a narrow enough subject that I won't be confusing.
6. I should aim my remarks at achieving the response I want from them.

QUESTION #3: HOW CAN I MAKE IT ENJOYABLE, INTERESTING, INFORMATIVE, AND PERSUASIVE?

1. I can prepare my speech thoroughly and deliver it enthusiastically.
2. I can collect all the information I need to explain, demonstrate, and convince the audience I know what I'm talking about.
3. I can select humor and warm stories that will spice it up and help to clarify my points.
4. I can select the material that appeals most to this audience at this time.
5. I can use persuasive language and illustrations.

QUESTION #4: HOW SHALL I ORGANIZE MY SPEECH?

1. First, I will go through all the material I've collected and select only that which is most relevant to this audience and to my speech.

2. Next, I will write out one concise sentence that clearly tells what I'm going to say. This will become my topic sentence.

3. Then I will reduce my ideas to three or four sentences that will clearly present the idea expressed in my topic sentence. I will arrange them in the most convincing order, and they will become my outline.

4. To fill out the outline, I will add explanations, supportive information, funny lines and stories, and persuasive points.

5. I will select a humorous, related story to use for my introduction and a brief summation for my main points to use for my conclusion. I will end my speech with a clear, convincing challenge for specific action.

6. Finally, I will let it ripen in my mind and heart until I understand the implications of everything I will say, am sure every point is as clear and convincing as I can make it, and I feel it very deeply.

**QUESTION #5: HOW CAN I PREPARE MYSELF
TO MAKE A GOOD DELIVERY?**

1. I will learn my outline well enough that I can remember it without notes.

2. I will practice until I feel comfortable expressing every point.

3. I will practice my gestures and expressions in front of a mirror or videotape recorder until they look and feel natural.

4. I will practice speaking until my voice sounds warm, convincing, and sincere.

5. I will practice until I could deliver my speech in a tornado.

**QUESTION #6: HOW CAN I KEEP MY COOL
WHEN I'M MAKING MY SPEECH?**

1. I will remember that stage fright is normal; that everybody gets it.

2. I will remember that stage fright is uncomfortable, but almost never fatal.

3. I will realize that almost nobody in the audience will notice I'm scared—unless I make a big deal of it.

4. I will concentrate on what I'm doing and saying; not on how scared I am.

5. I will stand erect, not lean on the lectern, breath deeply, and use my energy for constructive purposes like smiling, gesturing, and getting the audience involved.

QUESTION #7: HOW WILL I CONNECT WITH MY AUDIENCE AND KEEP THEM INVOLVED?

1. I will look my best and charm my audience with my personal warmth.
2. I will look, talk, and act enthusiastic.
3. I will use simple, straightforward, and strong language.
4. I will say every word distinctly—and with much expression.
5. I will watch my audience to make sure they are comfortable, interested, and involved.
6. I will make eye contact with individual people in my audience—particularly a few who look like they're enjoying my speech.
7. I will get my audience to do things with me.
8. I will get as physically close to my audience as I comfortably can.
9. I will test the microphone before I start and speak directly into it.
10. I will use humor again and again throughout the talk.
11. I will watch the time, knowing that the one mistake an audience won't forgive is my talking too long.
12. I will change pace often to keep the audience on the edge of their seats.

QUESTION #8: WHAT BARRIERS TO COMMUNICATION MIGHT I EXPERIENCE, AND HOW CAN I DEAL EFFECTIVELY WITH THEM?

1. There are physical barriers like discomfort and fatigue, which I can counter with the following strategies:

   - Plan for comfortable seating and needed breaks
   - Watch for signs of restlessness or drowsiness
   - Get the audience involved through physical exercises like clapping games

2. There are environmental barriers such as uncomfortable temperatures, an unsuitable meeting place, an inadequate public address system, and bad lighting. To counter them, I will:

   - Have someone keep tabs on the room temperature
   - Make sure there are enough chairs, but also assure that there are not enough extra chairs to make the room look empty and destroy intimacy
   - Test the P.A. system in advance, then make sure everyone can hear me
   - Ensure lighting that is bright enough to enable me to observe my audience

3. There are barriers like disinterest, competition from distractions, and biases that will cause the audience to resist hearing me. I will:

- Make sure that I know my audience well enough to interest them.
- Eliminate any distractions I can in advance and try to turn interruptions into humorous audience experiences.
- Use no humor that is offensive to audience members (such as ethnic jokes or remarks), establish early my authority to speak on the subject, and be very convincing in my presentation.

QUESTION #9: HOW CAN I MAKE CLEAR COMPLEX IDEAS, MAKE CONVINCING CONTROVERSIAL CLAIMS, AND MAKE INTERESTING OTHERWISE DULL MATERIAL?

1. I can use visuals (slides, handouts, objects, etc.) to appeal to the audience's highly developed sense of sight.
2. I can use images in my language that are vivid, clear, and appealing to the audience.
3. I can define my terms and use enough explanatory information to support my claims.
4. I can use humor to enliven dull material.
5. I can get audience feedback to make sure they understand everything I'm presenting.

QUESTION #10: HOW WILL I GET THE RESPONSE I DESIRE FROM MY AUDIENCE, AND HOW WILL I KNOW WHEN I GET IT?

1. I will state clearly and specifically what I want that audience to do.
2. I will repeat it several times to make sure they understand.
3. I will design feedback mechanisms to let me know exactly how successful my presentation was.
4. I will design follow-up feedback mechanisms to tell me how successful my message was.
5. I will follow through afterward to make sure that the people not only heard me clearly, but did what I wanted.

HOW TO BUILD
A POWERFUL STAGE PRESENCE

"When I stand up, my mind sits down!"

Why has that opening statement been used by so many amateur speakers over the years? It's probably because it represents pretty much what happens to many people when they stand before a group—particularly for their first few speeches.

Face it: most people are not accustomed to speaking while standing.

Everything changes when you are the only person standing in a group of people—even with people you know very well. Try it tonight: go home and stand in front of your family while you're telling them about your day. You'll see that it changes the way they relate to you, it changes the way you talk, and it changes the way you feel about what you are saying and the way you are saying it.

Standing in front of a group probably makes you nervous; even if you are usually perfectly at home with the same people while seated. When you stand up to speak, you become the center of attention. That makes most people nervous; and tension does strange things to most of us.

Yet it is this very position—the center of attention—that gives you the opportunity to get across what you want to say. Take away the root cause of the stage fright, and you also lose your opportunity to communicate effectively.

It is at this point, more than any other, that you can tell the difference between the amateurs and the professional speakers. The amateurs either give in to the stage fright and blunder through what they have to say, or look for ways of overcoming it—or hiding it. But the professionals turn the situation that causes the stage fright into the power to convey their ideas.

This making the most of being the center of attention is called stage presence. Instead of concentrating on their fear of failure, or their fear that the audience will reject them, experienced speakers concentrate on putting power into their stage presence.

If the audience wants to see a show (and most audiences do), they'll give them a show! If the audience wants to be entertained (and most audiences do), they'll entertain them! If the audience wants to be informed (and most audiences do) they'll inform them! Whatever that audience wants, the experienced speaker will do his or her best to give it to them!

There are three ways you can put power in your stage presence; and they are all captured in this oft-spoken advice:

- Stand up to be seen,
- Speak up to be heard and understood,
- And shut up to be appreciated.

Let's look more closely at each one, because together they hold the secret to a powerful stage presence.

STAND UP TO BE SEEN

What an audience sees has more impact than any other combination of factors on what they believe and receive from a speaker.

Now, that's a strong statement, and one that's hard to believe; but it is supported by modern research and years of personal experience.

Several years ago, Dr. Albert Mehrabian, a UCLA communications researcher, startled the communications field with findings of his extensive research on what makes an impact on audiences and what they believe in his book, *Silent Messages*. According to Dr. Mehrabian, there are three elements to spoken communications, and each has an impact on what audiences receive and believe. Look at how they stack up:

- Verbal messages—what you say—account for 7 percent of what is believed.
- Vocal messages—the way you say it—account for 38 percent.
- Visual messages—what the audience sees—account for a whopping 55 percent of what an audience believes.

In other words, more than half of your impact as a speaker depends on how you look to an audience and what that audience sees you do. If you question this, notice how you evaluate what a person says by the clothes that person is wearing, his or her gestures and mannerisms, and other visible factors.

I like to have fun with this insight; so I played a little trick on some automobile salespeople recently. I waited until almost closing time, then walked into a Mercedes dealership in a neighboring town. I wore some old jeans, a faded shirt, and sneakers with holes in them; and I had about a three-day growth of whiskers. When I walked in, all the salespeople glanced at me and went right on talking among themselves. Finally, the newest guy on the sales force was "elected" to come over and see what I wanted. All the other salespeople snickered when they overheard me say I might be interested in a new Mercedes.

165

"That guy'll learn someday how to size up a prospect," I heard one of them say.

Two days later, I gave that young man a check for *two* automobiles. (I understand there was a serious discussion at the next sales meeting of that dealership on the subject of how to qualify prospects.)

The point of all this is that people listen to what you say and believe what you say more than half the time merely on the basis of the way you look and what they see you do.

If you want to be heard and believed, *Stand up*—and that means a whole lot more than assuming an upright position.

First, it means stand up on the inside. Believe in yourself: believe you have something worthwhile to say, and that you have the ability to say it.

Second, it means stand tall. Look your best: dress your best, walk with confidence, stand erect, and act like you belong there. After all, you do!

Third, standing up means up take charge. Establish your authority early: give the person who introduces you enough information to present you as one who has something important to say, get the group to do something to show that you're in control, and look them squarely in the eyes. Don't be cocky, just take charge!

Fourth, Be natural. Be yourself: you are most convincing when you are real.

Fifth, when you stand up, you involve your audience. Play the host: I like to do it through quick, snappy games and exercises. (I'll use ten or twelve in a forty-five-minute speech.) I'm convinced that audiences love to be involved; and when they are, they'll listen to more of what you say, and believe more of what they hear.

Sixth, standing up means you get people to laugh. Don't just tell a funny story to kick off your talk—everybody will go to sleep when it's over. Sprinkle humor through your whole speech. Use one-liners, tell funny stories, do funny things—they'll love it! And they'll hear you better!

Seventh, When you stand up, you get visual. Be active, move around, use gestures, use visual aids and props, and, if possible, get into the audience. When you become a real live human being to them, they will listen, and they will believe you.

SPEAK UP TO BE HEARD
AND UNDERSTOOD

What you say does not have nearly the impact of the way you say it! If you want to be heard and understood—and believed—you've got to speak up.

Do you believe what you have to say? Does it matter to you? Is it important for your audience to hear? Then show it! Say what you have to say as if nothing in the world matters more to you at that moment!

Remember, what you say accounts for only 7 percent of the impact and believability of your presentation; the way you say it accounts for thirty-eight percent of what that audience hears and believes.

If you want to be heard, understood, and believed, *Speak up*—and that means a whole lot more than exercising your lungs, mouth, and vocal chords.

First, speaking up means you talk to be heard. Leave no doubt in any person's mind as to any word you've said: enunciate clearly, use the microphone and talk loudly enough to be heard in the back of the room, and test often to make sure you are being heard. If they don't hear it, they can't believe it!

Second, when you speak up, you use expression. Be convincing: put yourself into everything you say, vary your tone and volume level, and use pauses for effect. If you believe it, make them believe it.

Third, to speak up you have to get excited. Be enthusiastic: if something is wonderful, say it like it's wonderful; if something's sad, say it like it's sad; if something's important, tell it like it's important. They won't capture all that enthusiasm, but it's for sure they won't capture any more of it than you demonstrate to them!

Fourth, to speak up is to put yourself completely into what you say. Use your whole body: Show *big* with *big gestures,* show *little* with *little gestures,* show *action* with *movement.* Ham it up; your audience will love it!

Fifth, when you speak up you are using rhythm. Pace for interest and effect: change moods often, follow a strong point with a funny story, give your audience time to react, make it flow. Keep 'em on the edges of their seats all the time!

Sixth, speaking up means you speak to, not at, your audience. Zero-in on that audience: look into the eyes of one person for a few seconds, then move on to another; select several people who look like they're having fun and talk directly to them; tactfully play with individuals in the audience. Let 'em know you came to talk to *them!* After all, they came to hear *you!*

Seventh, when you speak up, you leave them loving you. Give them a grand finale: end your speech with your strongest and most dramatic story, tell them exactly what you want them to do, get them to join you in doing something for the close. Leave them applauding because they feel inside what you've been telling them!

SHUT UP TO BE APPRECIATED

Brevity is the very heart of a good speech. Many a good speech has been ruined by failure of the speaker to shut up while he or she was ahead.

"The brain can only contain, while the seat can remain," is one of my favorite reminders of the necessity of quitting before I wear out my welcome.

But there is a whole lot more to brevity than knowing when to end a speech. It begins with the first remark and runs like a thread through the whole speech. Here's a little of what it means to shut up to be appreciated.

First, shutting up means you do things quickly. Get to the point, get it said, and get out: don't spend any more time than necessary warming up your audience, don't drag out your stories, and don't talk too long about any one point. Allow only enough time for each event in your speech!

Second, to shut up is to know more than you tell. Don't tell everything you know about a point: tell enough to make it clear, then move on to something else. Discipline *yourself* to follow your schedule—not your audience!

Third, shutting up is knowing when you are through. Let your audience tell you when you're through: test to make sure they've caught each point, then move on. Your task is to speak, and the audience's task is to listen; make sure you finish yours before they finish theirs!

Fourth, to shut up is to quit when you finish, or when the

time comes. Nothing is more appreciated than a speaker who stops when he or she is through, or when the time is gone—whichever comes first. It's simple; just stop!

TYING IT ALL TOGETHER

You speak like a pro, even if you're an amateur. You can put power in your speech by using these principles:

1. Know your audience and play to them like a good actor plays to a full house.
2. Know your subject and present it in a clear, lively, and interesting manner.
3. Prepare well and practice, practice, practice.
4. Connect with your audience by caring about them more than you care about what you say.
5. Engage your audience in dialog through feedback.

GROWTH EXERCISE

Take an upcoming speech you must make and mentally process it through each of the questions and answers I have given. Plan now to cover every point mentioned in this chapter.

CHAPTER FIFTEEN

HOW TO WRITE TO GET ACTION

"Put it in writing!"

That order might scare you half to death because you feel:

- Writing something down immortalizes your words.
- It commits you—sometimes in a legally binding way.
- What's written can be ignored easier than what is said in person.
- You feel it might be misinterpreted.
- You might feel you don't do it very well.

Since some of us have to write letters, memos, and other correspondence from time to time, learning to do it well could pay big dividends. In fact, good correspondence can often make you money, get somebody off your back, or get something important done for you.

So, how can you write with confidence?

PLAN BEFORE YOU WRITE

Good letters, memos, and notes don't just happen—they're planned. Before you write the first word:

1. Decide what you want. Write it down in a concise statement. Pin it down exactly. "I want my money back!"

2. *List every point you want to cover.* If you're answering a letter, list all the answers you need to give. By the way, answer letters as quickly as you can—even if all you can say is, "I'm looking for your answers."

3. *Organize the points.* Number them according to their logical sequence. Arrange them in the most convincing manner.

4. *Make a rough draft.* Almost anything can be improved by rewriting.

WRITE WITH POWER AND ENTHUSIASM

Write it with the reader in mind.

1. *Personalize it.* Address it to a human being—not a "Sir" or a title. Write everything as if you're sitting across the desk, talking to the person. Write it from that person's point of view.

2. *Be positive.* Focus on benefits (what's in it for the person), rather than negative statements.

3. *Be pleasant.* Even if you're angry, talk nicely. You don't have to be ugly to be firm—and nice words are always easier to swallow if you have to eat them later.

4. *Use safe language.* Avoid saying anything you'd chuckle after saying in person. Tongue-in-cheek is hard to pull off in writing. Also, jargon is often confusing—and it can look very cold in type.

5. *Be concise.* Get to the point, say it, and get out. I won't ramble on about this.

6. *Don't play games.* Tell the reader what you want in the opening paragraph. If you try to be coy, the reader might file your letter in the "later" file without even reading it.

7. *Make it interesting.* Of course it's the message that's important; but you don't want your readers to think you're from the IRS. Even an unpleasant message can be written in a pleasant way. Don't add the misery of dull reading to an undesirable message.

8. *Make it brief.* "Please pardon the length of this letter," said a famous Frenchman of a bygone century, "but I didn't have time to make it shorter." It's not how long it takes you to write it that matters; it's how long it takes the person to read it. A page is maximum. If it takes more space, write an enclosure.

MAKE THEM WANT TO READ IT

Make it appetizing. Make everything about your correspondence jump out at the reader and say, "READ ME!" Remember, your letter represents you. If you always comb your hair, get rid of your bad breath and body odor, and look your best when you make a personal call, treat your letter similarly.

1. *Use an attractive letterhead.* Keep your letterhead simple and make sure it shows your best side. If you don't have a letterhead, use top-quality stationery—8½" by 11".

2. *Keep it clean.* Always type it. No typos, no erasures, no smudges. Sloppy letters say you're a sloppy person; or that you don't care much about the message.

3. *Spell correctly.* Nothing makes you look more ignorant than misspelling words. If you're not *absolutely sure,* take the time to look it up. It'll save you the time needed to overcome the poor impression later.

4. *Make it easy to read.* Vary the length of your sentences; but mostly keep them short. Keep paragraphs short, too. Lots of white space makes reading look easier and feel faster.

5. *Dress it up.* If it's important, *underline it.* If it's really important, *USE CAPITALS AND UNDERLINE IT!* And, don't be afraid to hit it with an exclamation point occasionally! Of course, don't overdo it—they'll miss the fine print.

6. *Use reader aids.* If the material is complex, you can help the reader get through it by using: 1) numerals to set aside a list, 2) outlines to show relationships, 3) indented margins to set off quotes or major points.

7. *Don't be pretentious.* A picture of yourself on your letterhead, an excessive use of "I" in writing or outlandish boasts will say "This letter's about *me,*" rather than "There's something in this letter for you!" The biggest question in the reader's mind is always, "What's in it for me?"

Write so that people know what you mean—write as much like you talk as you can. If you start out a conversation with "Re yours of 8/17/83, subject warranty," then start your letters that way: otherwise, don't.

1. *Be real.* Write so a person will know it's from you. Use plain talk—the language you and your reader know best.

2. *Be cordial.* Play the host. If you're funny in person, be funny in writing. Make the reader feel at home and glad to be there with you. Let your natural warmth come through.

3. *Be accurate.* Get your facts straight and stick to what you know to be true. If you want to give an opinion, that's okay; but make sure you label it as what you think. The slightest misrepresentation or exaggeration will make your reader question everything else you say.

4. *Prove it.* Avoid outlandish claims unless they are absolutely necessary. Truth is sometimes harder to believe than fiction. If it sounds too good to be true, prove it; if you don't, they won't believe it.

5. *Be direct.* Say what you mean. The professor said, "Previous ostentatious displays preclude such an acquisition," when his wife asked for a new fur coat. "I don't get it," his wife replied. "That's right, honey," he concluded. Well, why didn't he say that in the first place?

6. *Use active words.* Say it with nouns and verbs: avoid unessential adjectives and adverbs. Prefer the short word to the extended expression. Use ordinary words instead of linguistic articulations. Use words that act rather than words so lazy as to be thought passive.

7. *Specify.* Don't beat around the bush with hints and generalizations: say precisely what you mean. "We'll fire anybody we catch stealing!" is a lot clearer than "Persons suspected of misappropriation of funds will be dealth with in accordance with the company's policy regarding such matters."

The most crucial part of your letter is the ending: that's the moment of decision for the reader. Make it the strongest part of the letter.

1. *Make it clear what you want.* "I want an appointment with you" and "Please call me as soon as you have read this proposal" are clearer than "I hope you'll consider this and grant me an opportunity to explain it to you in more detail at some future time."

2. *Make clear when you want it.* If you ask someone to do it at their "earliest convenience," that's probably when you'll get it done. Ask for it when you want it: "We're on a tight schedule; so please put it on my desk by 8:00 A.M., next Monday."

3. *Close with a benefit.* "As soon as I get your okay, I can send you what you asked for." Make it attractive for your reader to do what you want done. But, remember, benefits are for your reader— not for you!

4. *Close like yourself.* If you end a conversation with "Very sincerely your humble servant," then sign your letters that way. Otherwise, get into the twentieth century with something like "Good luck" or "Be kind to yourself." Of course, if you don't know the reader, you'd better stick with something most people accept, like "Sincerely."

5. *P.S., Don't.* Avoid a P.S. if at all possible. It makes it look like you needed to rewrite the letter, but didn't think it important enough to spend the time doing it. Use a P.S. only to promise another letter (or a phone call) on an unrelated subject—and then only if you think the person expects some action on it.

HOLD ON! THERE'S ONE MORE BIGGIE!

Now that you've written the letter, there are three ways you can make it better.

First, if it's really important to you, let it ripen a while; then look it over carefully to make sure it says exactly what you mean in precisely the way you want to say it. If you feel it's not persuasive enough, or clear enough, or urgent enough, rewrite it.

Second, edit mercilessly. Cross out words that don't say anything, strike sentences that aren't really needed, and eliminate whole paragraphs you can do without. Change empty words to words full of life and meaning, change "fuzzy" words to words that are crystal clear, and long words to short ones. Count to see if you have used "you" at least three times for each time you've said "I." Turn it loose only when it says what you mean with all the force you desire!

Third, read it aloud twice. The first time, put in all the tones, pitches, and volume changes you'd use if you were saying exactly what's on the paper. Make sure it sounds like you. The second time, read it as flatly as you can. Remember, your reader will not have the benefit of your velvet voice or your glowing presence. When it sounds good, even when you read it without expression, you've got a winner.

TYING IT ALL TOGETHER

If you'll write like you talk to people, they'll understand what you mean, they'll enjoy reading your letter, and they'll be more likely to do what you want them to do.

I hope you get a lot more action out of your letters after applying what I've said in this chapter. Bet you knew most of it, anyway! (But sometimes it helps us to be reminded.)

GROWTH EXERCISE

Take a copy of a letter you've written and read over it to see how many of the things in this chapter you remembered to do. Rewrite it to reflect some of the ideas we've talked about.

CHAPTER SIXTEEN

HOW TO WRITE WELL FOR PUBLICATION

Good writers always do three things:

- They convey an idea,
- They create a feeling,
- And they provide a benefit for their readers.

That's true whether they're writing copy for an ad, or an article for a magazine, or a book. And if you can do these three things, you can write for publication.

Really, it's not easy; but it's easier than you might think—if you're willing to pay the price. That price must be paid in two installments:

First, you must be willing to follow some simple guidelines, which I'll give you in this chapter.

Second, you must be willing to think things through until you understand them. That means you have to work hard at it.

How much work does it take to be good at writing? The wise Emerson said, "There is no way to success in our art [writing] but to take off your coat . . . and work like a digger on the railroad, all day and every day."

Of course, you don't have to work at it *that* hard; unless you want to be very good at it. But you will find that the harder you work at writing, the easier it will become to you.

Since how hard you work at it will be determined by how

much you want to do it, I'll leave that with you and spend the remainder of my space on the basic guidelines that tell you how to do it.

START WITH THE MESSAGE

That might sound strange to you because most of us have been brainwashed to start with words. You know: "If you want to become a good writer, build a big vocabulary."

Horsefeathers! If words, or combinations of words, were all it took to write clearly and interestingly, computers could do it. It's ideas, thoughts, meanings, feelings, and messages that give writing its appeal and clarity. Nobody would care how good a way with words Erma Bombeck had if she didn't have some perfectly delightful things to say every time she puts together a column.

Writing is a lot like talking to someone. An empty-headed conversation goes like this: "Hi!" "How are you?" "Fine! How are you?" "I'm okay!" "Nice day, huh?" "Yeah! Nice day!" Then, there's a long, uncomfortable pause.

But strike up a conversation with a real live wire, and it's a totally different matter. You each stimulate the other to think, and can get so carried away that you have to discipline yourselves to keep from rambling all over the place. Time flies (it always does when you're having fun) and you have a hard time breaking away.

Now, there are three big differences between writing and talking to someone:

First, you have to get yourself going. You have to look into your background, or what's going on around you, or what other people are doing to start your thinking. You have to refine your thoughts into clear ideas.

Second, you have to discipline yourself to connect the ideas together into a message that makes sense.

Third, you have to give that message meaning. You have to translate the image you see in your mind into something the reader can see—and you have to make that reader care about what you have to say.

Sounds complicated? It's really quite simple, because there are some easy steps that can lead you right to it.

If you were taking a trip, you'd first decide where you wanted to go. Right? Likewise, you can't write clearly until you know what you want to say.

It's not enough to have a general idea of what you want to say. (Think of it as knowing the exact street address you want to reach.)

Let me illustrate that because this is the most important step you'll need to take. Perhaps you want to write an article about outer space. That's nice, but outer space is mighty big. So, you pin it down. You decide to write about astronauts traveling into space. That's better, but you could write a whole library on it—and still not cover the subject. Finally, you narrow it down to how a particular astronaut prepared mentally for a flight into space. Now you've got something you (and your readers) can get your teeth into.

One thing remains—but it's a big one. You must decide exactly what you wish to say about your subject. Here are some questions that can make that decision easier:

- What do you know best about it?
- What do you find most interesting about it?
- What do your readers know about it?
- How curious are they about it?
- What is the benefit for the reader in what you know?

Once you have a clear picture of the message you want to get across, boil it down into one concise sentence. That becomes your central theme. Grab it, like a bird grabs a worm, and don't let go of it until you have finished the entire article.

A good central sentence for your astronaut story could be: "We can take the fear out of a scary new experience by preparing as the astronaut did."

See? We've taken some random thoughts about a subject we, and our readers, are interested in and know something about; and we've woven it into a concrete idea we can present. From there, we can help our readers connect with the fears the astronaut felt, how he or she dealt with those fears, and how all of us can deal with scary new challenges the same way.

You can do it with any subject.

Step #2: Collect All the Ideas and Information You Can

The more you know about a subject, the better you can write about it. Ideas and information are like the water in a tank: you may need only a bucket full, but the more water there is in the tank the greater the force with which it will pour out.

Read everything you can get, talk to anybody who knows something about the subject, and try to get an interview with anybody who can give you good information or insights.

Write down anything you might quote, any illustrations you find, and all of the ideas that come to you while you're researching. It's a good idea to write it all on 3″ by 5″ index cards—one idea to a card. (We'll see why when we get to the next step.)

While you're collecting material, don't worry about how much of it you'll be able to use: just squirrel it away and keep thinking about how it all relates to your central theme.

Gradually, you'll begin to feel like you're getting a handle on it.

Step #3: Select and Organize Your Message

Here's where the self-discipline comes in. Go through the index cards on which you've written all those great ideas and pull out the three or four that seem to contain the strongest points.

That's right! Those three or four points will become your outline. It may feel like you're deserting some of your children: but it's the only way you can select what's important enough to include. Any more than four major points, and your writing will be so scattered your readers won't be able to follow you—unless, of course, you're experienced enough not to need this chapter.

Put all the other cards aside for now; you can use some of them later. Juggle the main point cards you've selected until they fall into a logical sequence. Keep words like these in mind as you shuffle the cards: "first," "then," "how," and "therefore." Gradually, you'll see a connection between the points, and your outline will take shape.

It might look something like this:

I. An astronaut's first flight can be scary—like our lives.
II. To do anything worthwhile, you have to overcome fears.
III. Here's how the astronaut did it.
IV. You can take the fear out of life's new experiences the same way.

With an outline like that you can convey an idea, you can create a feeling, and you can provide a benefit for the reader—if you'll follow the outline like a road map.

Step #4: Fill in the Outline

Go back through the cards you've laid aside and look for information and ideas that can help you explain, prove, clarify, and make your readers feel what you want to say in your central theme and main points.

Look for good mini-stories (people love stories), look for strong images (mental pictures help people see your points), and look for simple and clear explanations (they help people understand). Don't get carried away with it, though: one good illustration or image is usually enough to make each point clear. Any more than two, and you'll confuse your readers. And make sure that the one you choose to explain each point fits that point like a glove fits a hand.

You'll be tempted to hang onto some of the little jewels you have written on those cards because they are so utterly charming, or you feel so strongly about them, or you had such a hard time getting them. However, if you're really serious about writing clearly and interestingly, you must let them go unless they are essential, and they really fit the main point.

Arrange the cards behind their appropriate main point cards, and you have your outline.

Read over the outline until you pick up the flow of ideas. Keep coming back to the central theme you wrote down first. Go over it until you really feel it.

Now you're ready for the final step in preparation.

Step #5: Decide How
You Will Start and Stop

How will you grab the browsing reader's attention? How will you introduce the subject and draw the reader into it? How will you alert the reader that there's something in the article for him or her?

You can do it with a strong introduction. For instance, you could tell a mini-story that makes the reader feel what the astronaut felt. If you choose that approach, build the mini-story on conflict—the kind of stuff they build Saturday morning cartoons around. It's a strong grabber. But make sure the conflict touches the kind of feeling your reader can identify with.

Another good introduction is a strong quote that ties the whole article up into a powerful sentence. Again, make the reader feel connected with the speaker.

Or you can simply open with a strong statement. You might say something like: "Climbing on top of a thousand-foot Roman candle pointed toward the stars is scary business—like facing a big operation, or starting a new job, or sometimes just facing the dailiness of life."

A good introduction sets the reader up to expect some benefit from getting on into the article, and it introduces the subject in an attractive way.

Now, at the other end of the article, you need a conclusion—an ending.

But a good conclusion does much more than hold up a "The End" sign. It reminds the reader of your main idea, it locks in the feeling you want to get across, and it leaves the reader feeling good about having read what you have written.

Sounds like a big order, doesn't it? Well, it is, and it might take a lot of time; but it's not hard. The easiest way to write a conclusion is to sum up your main idea and the reader's benefit in a short paragraph or sentence. Another way is to draw a conclusion after some words like, "So you see. . ." or "Therefore. . . ." Or you can simply send the reader off with a wish for a happier life based on the benefit your article has given. Actually, there are many ways you can do it.

What's important is that you know your conclusion *before* you write the first word. I know that sounds strange; but the only way to write clearly is to know where you are going before you take the first step.

So you can see that most of the sweat comes before you begin writing. You have to decide what you will say before you can say it. Next, you have to decide how you will say it. If you do those things well, the rest is easy.

It's this simple: if you have something important and interesting to say, you can find a way to say it. If you don't, the words won't mean a thing.

MOVE ON TO SENTENCES

Ideas and feelings are expressed through sentences.

Of course, we use words to make those sentences; but words only have meaning when they stand in relation to other words. For example, the word "yes" can stand as a whole sentence, and it conveys a very strong message; but it means nothing unless it is connected to a question.

So, what is a sentence? It is an idea, thought, or feeling put into words.

Keep in mind that it's sentences the readers try to grasp. This is particularly true as more and more people are learning to speed-read. So, the easier you make it for readers to grasp ideas by the way you put words together, the better your readers can understand what you mean.

The best way to help readers understand what you mean is to use plain talk. Terse, clear, picturesque expressions of ideas— that's plain talk. It's the language of the people. When we use plain talk, we simply try to say what we think. When we write like most of our readers talk, they can get what we mean.

How do you write plain-talk sentences? Here are some tips you might find useful:

Tip #1: Use Easy-to-Read Sentences

Short sentences are easier to read than long ones. Those with eight words or less are easiest to read. The difficulty of reading a sentence goes up in direct ratio to the number of words it contains.

Does that mean you should only use short sentences? Not at all! Most people can handle fifteen to seventeen words quite well. What works best is to vary the length of the sentences: it makes what you write more pleasant to read.

The best way to make what you write easy to read is to try to write like most of your readers talk. Wouldn't you rather have people understand what you say than to have them admire the way you say it?

One caution: Don't try to "write down" to your audience. The old idea that you must write for a twelve-year-old mentality is insulting; besides, it's almost impossible to do it well. It takes a lot more than writing skills to reach children.

Tip #2: Use Familiar Word Combinations

Franklin D. Roosevelt's speech writer once wrote: "We are endeavoring to construct a more inclusive society." F.D.R. changed it to read, "We're going to make a country in which no one is left out."

Don't throw high-sounding words at it—say it! Interestingly, familiar phrases are usually shorter and more direct—that's probably why they are more familiar to us.

Jargon is useful *only* when you are writing to a very specialized audience. For example, a marine biologist might write for other scientists, "The biota exhibited a 100 percent mortality response." Most of us would be better off saying, "All the fish died."

Studies have shown that most people like the pages they are looking at to look much like pages they have seen before. If people are familiar with the way things are being said, they can concentrate more on what is meant. Who benefits most when your readers understand what you mean? You!

Another caution: Avoid familiar phrases if they don't say anything. Here's a little list of empty phrases to avoid:

for the purpose of	instead of	for
from the point of view of	instead of	for
in order to	instead of	to
with reference to	instead of	about
in the event that	instead of	if

Tip #3: Use Good Grammar, But Don't Let It Enslave You

Good grammar is usually best because it is almost always the clearest way to say things. That's how it got to be good grammar. The better you know the rules, the more clearly you can write.

The rules are to help, not hinder—like the rule that says a preposition must always be placed before the word it governs. That rule is there so you say things clearly: not to force you to say things awkwardly.

For example, Winston Churchill received a hot letter from an angry schoolteacher who was protesting Parliament's poor use of English in writing some of its laws. "Why they are even misplacing prepositions!" she wrote. "Madame," Sir Churchill agreed, "this is an outrage up with which we will not put!"

Grammar is a little like the United States Constitution—very important, but in constant need of interpretation. Violate the rules if you must; but only when it is necessary to protect ideas, meanings, and clarity. Now, that's a rule you can work with!

Tip #4: Use Punctuation to Direct the Reader

Readers need a lot of help to follow what you say. They look to your punctuation like drivers look to road signs and signals to tell them how to drive. Good punctuation tells readers when to stop, or slow down, or speed up, or whatever they need to do to avoid the danger of losing your meaning.

Of course, you don't use punctuation when you talk. You use a system of pauses, volume and pitch changes, expressions, and even gestures to guide your listeners. Punctuation helps you guide your readers when you write.

Now some writers feel that punctuation is a necessary evil which should be used only when necessary no matter how complex their sentence structure so they use only periods at the ends of their sentences and an occasional comma but aren't even sure when they should do that while others are so lazy that they have never taken the time to learn how to use anything but periods.

Only writers who want their readers to enjoy and understand what they write need to concern themselves with learning how to use punctuation effectively. Others can just stick to short sentences. Readers can follow them. So what if they slow you down? Who cares if reading is jerky? That is the reader's problem. Right? Wrong!

One reason so few people know enough about punctuation to use it well is that they've tried to learn it from English books that talk about "subjunctive clauses," "connectives," "declaratives," and such things. For formal writing, those things are good to know; but you don't need to know all of them to help your readers through a simple article. A few essentials can get you through. Since they are easier to learn if you associate them with something you already know, you can learn punctuation marks in a few minutes by comparing them with traffic signals.

The following chart might help:

HOW PUNCTUATION CONTROLS READING TRAFFIC

WHEN DRIVING IF YOU SEE:	YOU:	WHEN WRITING, YOU USE:
A green light	Go ahead at a safe speed	White space between words and paragraphs
A yellow light	Slow down	A comma
A red light	Stop	A period
A Railroad Sign	Stop and look both ways	A colon or semicolon
A flashing yellow light	Watch for the unexpected	A dash or parentheses
A flashing red light	Stop quickly and look carefully	An exclamation point
A flashing blue light	Pause to identify the source	Quotation marks
A siren	Pull over and pay close attention	Underline (italics), or all capitals
A merge traffic sign	Watch for vehicles coming together	A hyphen between words

Of course, there are some details you'll need to check—like the difference between a colon and a semicolon—but you can do that when you are editing. The important thing to remember is that you are trying to help the readers find their way through your ideas; not prepare a document for a panel of professors.

Tip #5: Use Your Own Style

Let your real personality come through in your writing. It's only newspaper reporters and technical writers who are trained to reveal nothing of themselves in their writing. With them, it's just the facts—nothing but the facts.

But readers of articles usually like to know what kind of person they're spending time with. It's the revelations about yourself—accidental or intentional—that come through when you write; this is called style.

The more real you are, the more likely the reader is to identify with what you say and to accept what you say. An honest and sincere style is always convincing. If you're funny in real life, let that humor come through when you write. It will make the reading more pleasant. If there are expressions you use often, it's probably because you understand them and think they are strong. Use them; they can help your readers understand your ideas. Just as in real life, the real you is the most enjoyable and believable.

Okay, so you start with the message, move on to sentences, and—at last—you're ready to start writing.

PUT IT INTO WORDS

Use words to say what you mean; but remember that they are not there to call attention to themselves. Words are the vehicles you use to carry your message, the bricks you use to build your message. The better they are, the less aware of them the reader is.

Does that mean that words are not important? Certainly not! Emerson suggested you use "words as hard as cannon-balls." Let's look at how he practiced what he preached. He said, "The years teach much which the days never know." There's not a fancy word in that sentence. All the words but one have only one syllable, and it has two. Yet, as simple as it is, that group of words has a lot of impact.

Just as you use words to express what you think, readers must use words to think what you express. The more you help them, the easier it is for them to grasp your ideas. It's only egomaniacs who throw around big words to impress people with how big their vocabularies are; good writers help their readers understand, feel, and see with their words.

Here are some guidelines that can help you do that:

1. Use simple words. Short words are better than long words, plain words are better than fancy words, and nouns and verbs are better than adjectives and adverbs. Use a complex word only if you can't find a simple word that will carry the meaning.

2. Use clear words. Jargon, slang, and folksy words serve to confuse. Use words that everyone who reads your writing can understand.

3. Use easy-to-read words. When a word is unfamiliar, or hard to pronounce, it slows the reader down. And a reader slowed down too often stops reading!

4. Use full words. Some words are just full of meaning—like "bureaucrat," "pregnant," and "go." They say more than "governmental supervisor," "gestating," and "proceed."

5. Use active words. Readers can move right along with active verbs. Passive words slow them down. You wouldn't say, "The Delaware was crossed by General Washington." Rather, you'd say, "General Wshington crossed the Delaware." Always make it active if you can.

6. Use vivid words. Say the word "slap," and you quickly form an image of an action. Some words even sound like what they mean. Listen as you say words like "bang," or "screech," or "slimy." Vivid words help your reader form images.

7. Use precise words. Concrete words help the reader to pin down exactly what you mean, but abstract words are hard to grasp. For example, "millions and millions of dollars expended" does not have the power of "six-point-two million dollars wasted."

8. Use words correctly. Learn the difference (or look up the difference) between troublesome words like effect and affect, or anxious and eager. Say precisely what you mean to say.

9. Avoid exaggerations. Superlatives—like "greatest," "best," and "most"—are particularly questionable. Sometimes the exaggeration is subtle—like saying "incredible" when you mean "outstanding." Use too many exaggerations and your whole message becomes suspect.

10. Be discreet. Use good taste in the words you choose and in the way you use them. In some publications, it is acceptable to say something like "He puked all over the place," but, generally, it is better to use the more restrained "He lost his dinner" or "He vomited."

Now comes the ultimate (that's no exaggeration) in self-discipline.

EDIT WITHOUT MERCY

Once you have written your article, go back over it with a fine-toothed comb. Read it as if you didn't write it, and look for every flaw in it.

First, check the overall flow of it. See if it's easy to read and understand.

Second, cut out every word, every sentence, every paragraph that is not really necessary.

Third, check and double-check. Check spelling, punctuation, definitions, meanings—everything. If *anything* looks questionable to you, check it out.

Finally, read it over carefully to see that everything about it is clear, readable, and attractive. Retype it, and check it for typos.

Most publications do their own editing, but the better it looks when they receive it from you, the more likely they are to publish it. Also, the more you polish it up, the fewer changes others will have to make in it.

TYING IT ALL TOGETHER

Good writing is mind-to-mind reorientation, and enjoyable reading is heart-to-heart identification.

Good writers always convey an idea, create a feeling, and provide a benefit for the reader. They start with a strong message, move on to concise sentences, say it with plain words, and edit without mercy.

When they have finished, they have created something that can be enjoyed, understood, believed, and acted upon. Most of all, they have provided their readers a benefit.

GROWTH EXERCISE

Reread an article in a major magazine—an article you especially enjoyed and look for evidence that the writer did the things we talked about in this chapter. Try to pick up the central message, notice the outline, study the sentences, look carefully at the words, and locate the promised benefit. After you've read it over, go through the first five paragraphs and see if you can cut out anything without losing the sense and flow of the writing.

CHAPTER SEVENTEEN

HOW YOU CAN WIN WITH TELEVISION

What can television do for you as a communicator? Probably much more than you realize.

It must be pretty powerful stuff, or big companies—which usually count paper clips—wouldn't keep going back year after year to tell their stories at a cost of $100,000 to $250,000 per commercial.

Maybe you don't have big bucks to spend on commercials; maybe advertising has little to do with the way you make your living; maybe you don't even like television—but don't go 'way just yet!

There might be some ways you can win big at the television game. Let's explore some of the opportunities it offers, some things you need to know about the medium if you're going to cash-in, and how you can make the most of what it offers you.

TV IS THE ONLY
MASS COMMUNICATIONS MEDIUM

Television is the only true mass medium of communication. That might sound like a big claim, but think about it.

First, television reaches more people on a daily basis than

any other medium—some claim it reaches more people than all other media combined.

Second, most newspapers and radio stations concentrate on much smaller geographical areas than do TV stations.

Third, other media go after a segment of "the market," but television programs for the masses of people.

Fourth, only television has an effective network system that connects the average person with events that are happening around the world—instantly.

But what does all this contact with people have to do with you as a communicator? People who learn how to plug into the mass of people, through television, find they can do things that are otherwise impossible—and sometimes at surprisingly little, or no, cost.

For example, I once spoke at a national management meeting for Broyhill Furniture Industries, Inc. As I talked with the top people in that company, I asked them how much money they had spent on network television commercials to gain their high visibility. I was amazed when they told me they had spent practically nothing.

Then I discovered their technique. Years ago, they had started giving suites of their furniture to nationally-televised game shows. The shows would give them away as prizes to their contestants. Now, since the game show hosts wanted to impress audiences with the value of the prizes the contestants were winning, they would always give the Broyhill name a big build-up.

So, everybody wins! The audience is entertained, the contestants win prizes, the shows get prizes for free, and Broyhill gets mass exposure for its name and products. Believe me, the cost of making a suite of furniture is nothing compared with the price of a television spot. Besides, if a contestant didn't win—and sometimes ten and fifteen in a row didn't—Broyhill got the exposure without even having to give the prize. No wonder they're still doing it!

Maybe you don't make furniture, but I'd bet there is something that is important to you that television could help you with. The key is in knowing what you want, and making television work for you to get it.

Let's look at some of the benefits contact with TV's vast audiences can give you:

You Can Gain Vast Exposure Free

Even if your dream is not to become a national celebrity, don't overlook some of the positive benefits of public exposure. There is tremendous power in being known by large numbers of people.

Talk show hosts are always looking for guests on their shows—people who are interesting, who've done or are doing things, or who have something interesting to say to their audiences. Since a lively guest helps their ratings, they will invite you to appear free. (We'll talk later about how to get an invitation.)

There are times that communicators do things that merit coverage on the news. Again, since the news shows look for stories that will inform or entertain their audiences, you get to appear free. (We'll also talk later about how to get on the news.)

I've appeared on local news shows and talk shows, and I've always been amazed at how many people later told me they had seen me.

Television Exposure Enhances Your Prestige

Some of the highest-paid people in this country are television personalities. The reason they are so highly paid is that their names and faces are recognizable by millions of people.

Masses of people sit up and take notice when a celebrity does, or says, something—almost anything. As a result, celebrities can easily get books published, champion worthwhile causes, endorse products, and do many other things that are simply not available to unknown people.

Television Can Help You Make Valuable Contacts

You never know who is going to be watching when you appear on television.

There are countless stories of how a person watched a person on television, made contact with that person, and helped him or her do something that was really important to both of them.

Also, television seems to attract people with resources. Another guest who appears with you on a talk show could prove to be a valuable person for you to know.

TV IS NOT FOR EVERYBODY

Of course, television is not for everybody. Each of us must decide how important it is for us and go from there. If you think appearing on television might help you reach some of your goals, there are some things about the medium that would help you to know.

TELEVISION IS A
UNIQUE COMMUNICATIONS MEDIUM

People who benefit from working with television put a great deal of effort into learning about the medium itself. Here, I can only mention a few of the more important aspects of the TV industry—things you need to know if you are going to try to break into it.

Television Is
An Entertainment Medium

TV programming has been attacked about as many times as anything in our society. It has been called "a vast wasteland," the "boob tube," and many other undesirable names by people who wanted to make it something other than what it has been. But the major networks, and most local stations, have understood from the very beginning that television is basically an entertainment medium. They know that most of the people who watch it, most of the time, do so to be amused.

Any time you approach a talk show host, think of yourself as entertainment. It's this simple: come up with a way to help enough people have fun watching you, and you can get on television. Try to make something else out of television and you're fighting a losing battle.

Television Programmers Are
Primarily Concerned With Ratings

The name of the television game is audience. Television programmers make all their money from commercials: the more people a show has in its viewing audience, the more commercials they can sell, and the higher the prices they can charge for them. Sound materialistic? It is; but it's the way it works!

The number of people watching a show is translated into "rating points," and the programmers work hard to get them, and they fight hard to keep them. Find a way to help a talk show host or news director boost his or her ratings, and you've got yourself a slot in a show.

Local Television Is Increasingly
Information Conscious

The revolution in electronics that has been going on for the last few years has opened up many new doors on a local level. Cable-TV, low power UHF stations, and "interactive systems" have all brought a new look to the face of television.

Many of the new channels are programming for very select audiences, and some of them are building their programming around information—with a flair for entertainment. Find a way to help these local stations compete more successfully with the larger stations, and with each other, and you can reach at least a small audience. Sometimes it can be a stepping stone to bigger and better things.

Television Is Visual

One way effective communicators have found to break into television is to develop a visual dimension to what they do. People must have something appealing to watch while they are listening to the sound. In fact, TV producers consider the visual impact more important than the sound impact. When the two work together, you've got a winner!

For example, some strong news stories get very little play because there is nothing the reporters can show while they are telling the story. Others that have very little news value get more time because they are visually appealing.

Any time you can help a TV producer come up with a strong visual appeal to what you want to do, you have a much better chance of getting on a show. When you can give a producer both visual image and a good sound appeal, you have something strong going for you.

Television Moves Fast

Most TV news stories last for about twenty seconds; even the big stories seldom run more than a minute. Anybody who has ever been on television knows that the scene changes every few seconds.

What that means for the communicator is that you must be able to do or say things fast. When you are on a talk show, there's no time to sit around and get a conversation going. The host asks a question, and you're off and running. You have to work at saying things quickly, concisely, and clearly.

Also, you have to be flexible enough to jump around. It's not unusual to be interrupted in mid-sentence for a commercial break or the introduction of a new guest. You may not like it— few people do—but you have to learn to work with it.

Television Is Beyond
Your Control Most of the Time

When you are a guest on a television show, you are at the mercy of the host or reporter. You can only answer the questions you are asked, in the amount of time they give you. As a result, many people who appear alert and alive on the stage come across on TV as slow and uncertain.

There are two keys to looking good under these circumstances: 1) prepare some questions for the host in advance, and 2) develop the agility to give strong answers quickly.

If you've never been on television you're in for an interesting experience. The place usually looks like an explosion in a TV equipment factory. There are lights, cameras, props of all kinds—many of them held together with clamps, wire, or tape. And there are countless people, doing all kinds of things.

In this mass of confusion, with frantic pace you're expected to look and sound intelligent, act natural, and communicate with an audience you can't see. It's a big order, but those who do it well can benefit greatly from it. It can even be fun.

Here are some tips to help you make the most of an appearance on television: First, prepare yourself.

- Know exactly what you want to accomplish.
- Know what you will say and do.
- Make notes for review just prior to going on the air.
- Learn as much as you can about the studio environment before you go in.
- Watch the show several times to pick up the flow, pace, and emphases.
- Prepare any graphics (slides, videotape, pictures, etc.) or demonstrations.
- Practice giving short, snappy, and lively answers.
- Practice any demonstrations you might use.

Second, prepare the show's host and producer.

- Send to the producer a short introduction showing one or two outstanding things the host might use to promote and introduce you. Be sure to include your name and title.
- Send the producer (well in advance) all details about graphics or demonstrations you plan to do. Most shows welcome good visuals because they add life to the show.
- Ask the producer for tips on how to prepare.
- Send a list of questions the host might ask you to get things rolling. Also, take a copy with you, in case the original gets lost.

Third, when you arrive in the studio, be ready.

- Look your very best. Choose clothes that are appropriate to your image and are color-keyed to the set. Avoid small prints, checks, plaids, whites: they are hard for viewers to watch.
- Communicate with the producer, director, host, and other personnel to make sure you understand what they want from you, and that they understand what you need done.
- Concentrate on what you are doing—not on how frightened you are.

Fourth, try to be your best self on the air.

- Try to be real. Don't imitate someone else, avoid using notes, and ignore all the confusion.
- Try to relax, but don't slump. Sit comfortably upright and stay alert.
- Talk to the host of the show and give short answers, but avoid starting each answer with his or her name. Look at the host.
- If you have to give longer answers or a demonstration, look directly into the camera with the red light (lighted) on top of it.
- If you hold anything up before the camera, make sure you hold it high enough for the camera to pick it up—and hold it very still.
- Be intimate. Talk as if you are talking to one person.
- Be animated. Use gesture and expressions as naturally as if you were carrying on a conversation with a close friend.
- Be fun. Smile, laugh, and be funny if you can. Remember, you're there to entertain.
- Always assume you are on camera unless you are told otherwise.
- Be pleasant, courteous to the host and other guests, and patient—no matter what happens.

Finally, make the most of the opportunity.

- Notify people within your organization that you will be appearing on television. It can be a good employee morale-builder.
- Publicize the show in your publications, among clients, in trade associations, etc. Even if people don't watch the show, it's nice for them to know you were on.
- Ask for a videotape of the show for future use. The station might make a slight charge for the tape and duplication, but it can be a valuable tool for marketing and future reference. You can also use it for review and improvement.

TYING IT ALL TOGETHER

As our world becomes increasingly oriented toward television, you might find it a useful vehicle for conveying your messages. If you can find ways to help TV producers and hosts boost their ratings, they will offer you valuable opportunities to connect with their vast audience.

GROWTH EXERCISE

Watch several talk shows to see if the guests follow through with the suggestions we've offered in this chapter. Note how, and why, they were selected to appear, what they do that looks and sounds good, and how they could improve. Look for evidence that television is basically an entertainment medium.

CONCLUSION

A television reporter asked the world-famous pianist, Arthur Rubinstein, in the closing years of his life, "Are you the greatest musician who ever lived, as some people have said?"

"Music is an art, not a science," said the wise old master, "and no one ever becomes the greatest at an art—they could always be greater!"

"Do you have any regrets?" the reporter then asked the pianist, who was nearing his death at age ninety-five.

"I'm ashamed to say this at the end of my life—which is now," the old man said after a long pause, "but there are many pieces I was never able to perform for an audience because I was too lazy to practice enough to do them well."

Communication is a lot like that—an art which all of us could perform better, and always perform better. And, just as the great Rubinstein, most of us are too lazy to become the best we could become.

He knew, as I know—and, as I suspect, you know—that the key to success is the sweat of practice. Yet, we all know that sometimes our practice can be helped along by knowledge. Sometimes we can learn from the success and failures of people who have gone before us and who willingly have shared what they have learned.

It is my hope that this book has helped you to shortcut some of the things that I and many others have learned only through experience and practice.*

And yet, I know that only you can determine how effective you will become as a communicator.

I leave you with a story to ponder. A little boy was accompanying his father, a circuit-riding preacher, on his round of little country churches one Sunday a hundred years ago.

When they entered the first church, the little fellow noticed that his father took out a penny and placed it in an offering box at the back of the church. The boy knew that people were expected to place their gifts in that box, and it was from these gifts that his father would be paid his meager salary.

When the service was over, the little boy watched as his father opened the box, looked in, and pulled out its contents—two pennies.

"Daddy!" said the boy, "If youda' put more in, youda' got more out!"

As a communicator, the more you put into it, the more you'll get out of it.

Good luck! I hope you get what you're after.

* A listing following the index provides information about my cassette albums available from Creative Services, Inc.

INDEX

203

Here's a listing of Nido Qubein's cassette albums available from Creative Services, Inc., P. O. Box 6008, High Point, North Carolina 27262, (919) 889–3010.

"Techniques of Professional Selling"

Here's an eight-cassette album that'll help you learn all the important basics in the world of selling. This practical step-by-step guide can make you a top salesperson. Nido Qubein calls on his personal experience as a professional sales trainer and a proven, successful salesman to share with you some of his dynamic principles. Packed in a handsome, sturdy vinyl binder, this program is worth being listened to again and again by both the novice and the professional. You'll get these sixteen different presentations recorded on eight cassettes: Increase Your Effectiveness, Build Your Sales Communications Skills, Add Power to Your Persuasion, Work Smarter—Not Just Harder, Manage Your Territory, Manage Your Opportunities, Become Your Company's Field Expert, Turn Knowledge into Sales, Play to the Customer, Discover the Power of Asking Questions, Focus on Maximum Effect, You Can Close With Confidence, Close like the Pros, Turn Objections into Sales, Turn Stalls into Action.   ($89)

"Success System"

With this eight-cassette series, Nido Qubein can help you to awaken your sleeping giant and to excel in your career. As a top professional speaker, Nido has shared the contents of this program with hundreds of audiences around the country. And here for your personal library are the dynamic principles which lead to successful living. This cassette program is a fast-moving, hard-hitting, factual presentation designed for use by a wide variety of individuals and groups. It is practical and meaningful. In a few hours, you too can discover how to possess the magic power of successful living. You'll get sixteen idea-packed sessions including: How to Enjoy a Winner's Attitude, How to Develop Self Confidence, How to Set and Monitor Your Goals, How to Manage Your Time Effectively, How to Be an Effective Leader, How to Motivate Yourself and Others, How to Conduct Productive Meetings, How to Put Off Procrastination, How to Handle Stress and Distress, How to Avoid Burnout.   ($89)

"How to Communicate Your Way to Success"

This cassette series by professional speaker Nido Qubein will help you to reach your potential in effective communication. I will share with you Nido's proven ideas which have brought him hundreds of engagements annually at very high fees. Do you long to be able to speak to an audience without being frightened half to death? Do you want to be able to speak so interestingly that your audience (whether one person or a thousand people) wants to hear you again? It's not as hard as you might think. Many people could do it better if they would follow the suggestions offered in this series. You'll get eight different cassettes which include these topics: You Can Become a More Effective Communicator, How to Target Your Audience, How to Prepare and Deliver Your Speech, How to Use Humor, How to Use the Telephone, How to Write Effectively, How to Lead Productive Meetings, How to Listen Creatively, and much more. ($89)

Save $42. Order all three albums for only $225.